"There is a difference between *knowing* and *believing* our true identity ~~in Christ.~~ Believing requires experiencing the truth we know. Dr. Wardle's *Identity Matters* provides not only the knowledge of our true identity, but also a practical pathway to experience the truth of it so that the reader may come to *believe* who they truly are in Christ. This is a classic in the making and an indispensable guide to the truest self in Christ."

> —**Dr. Thom Gardner,** adjunct professor of Spiritual Formation at Winebrenner Theological Seminary, International speaker and author of several books, including *Healing the Wounded Heart, The Healing Journey, Relentless Love, Living the God-Breathed Life,* and *Everything that Grows,* founder of Restored Life Ministry, Inc.

"I have been reading books by Terry Wardle for over thirty years. I love everything Terry writes, but *Identity Matters* has now become one of my favorites. Why? Because if you get the foundation right, everything else comes together. Get the foundation wrong and everything falls apart. Terry's book on Identity helps us get the foundation right. The truth in this book is transformational."

> —**Dr. Ron Walborn,** Vice President and Dean of Nyack College and Alliance Theological Seminary, Nyack, New York

"Within these pages, find a painting of personal spiritual renewal. Take in every life-giving detail. You will notice a firm canvas of sound theology framed carefully with ample Scripture. The sketch is Terry's own journey, carefully colored with raw vulnerability and heartwarming personal stories. The insights are clear, practical, and pastoral, inspiring us to live out our own portrait of who we are in Christ."

> —**Mark Ongley,** pastor, counselor, and author of *Into the Light: Healing Sexuality in Today's Church*

"In a society where true connection with others and true identity loss has led to epidemic substance abuse and loss of life, the material presented here tenderly and transparently by Dr. Wardle is a life line. If people know who they are, and whose they are, the possibility for health and healthy relationships is much greater. The practices and reflection questions in this book provide an onramp to the abundant life that is promised in Scripture."

> —**Michelle Dayton, MD,** Emergency Physician, Spiritual Director

"Dr. Wardle reminds us that without the solid foundation of identity, one's mental state can become captive to uncontrollable external and internal forces. Amen! Ivdentity is vital to a healthy mental state. Being solid in one's identity is the anchor that restores hope to the hopelessness of depression and anxiety. Although biochemical markers must often be addressed in treatment, we must not ignore the importance of pursuit of spiritual health in order to bring about balanced mental recovery. We have to treat the patient as a whole, and that must include spirit."

> —**Gina Glenn Hutton, MD,** Psychiatrist

"We've had trouble trusting God and believing in his best for us since the Garden–with horrific results. In *Identity Matters*, Dr. Wardle clearly identifies the tragic consequences of believing the cacophony of lies that inundate us. This is a compelling work that is sure to resonate with the deep-seated experiences of the reader. Dr. Wardle not only highlights the necessity of security in Christ, he also describes and encourages the journey towards experiencing it."

—**John Shultz,** Retired President, Professor Emeritus, Ashland Theological Seminary

"No one weaves personal story, biblical content, and practical application together better than Terry Wardle. I love this book! At times I smiled. At times I cried. Always, I felt the Holy Spirit talking to my soul. I plan to read *Identity Matters* to my family during our nightly devotions."

—**William P. Payne, PhD,** The Harlan & Wilma Hollewell Professor of Evangelism and World Missions, Director of Chaplaincy Studies, Ashland Theological Seminary

"*Identity Matters* goes straight to the heart of the African American struggle in America. Moreover, for the African American Christian, Terry has provided a rich resource for those who have to live with a triple consciousness of identity in a culture that began with defining them as 'chattel property.' Just the historical nomenclature of identification bespeaks the continuation of this multigenerational trauma that has resulted in the present division of these yet-to-be-United States. And unfortunately, the Christian church has not always been the 'balm in Gilead' to heal our sin-sick and divided souls. But God has sent us a Pastor and Prophet in the person of Terry Wardle with the gospel and this Gift of Grace in this transformational book. It's required reading for all who are on the Journey of Hope, Healing, and Wholeness."

—**Dr. Arlee Griffin Jr,** Senior Pastor of Berean Baptist Church, Brooklyn, NY, and Raleigh, NC, and Former President of American Baptist Churches, USA

"What stands in the way of us bringing our best selves to work, worship, and community relationships? In *Identity Matters,* Terry Wardle creates a stirring experience you do not want to miss. He leverages and intertwines scholarship, spiritual insight, personal stories, and transparency to provoke thought and provide application that addresses perhaps the greatest source of waste in our individual and organizational lives: failure to access our highest potential."

—**Joseph C. High,** SVP and Chief People Officer, W. W. Grainger, Inc.

Identity Matters

DISCOVERING

WHO YOU ARE

IN CHRIST

Terry Wardle

LEAFWOOD
PUBLISHERS

an imprint of Abilene Christian University Press

IDENTITY MATTERS

Discovering Who You Are in Christ

LEAFWOOD
PUBLISHERS
an imprint of Abilene Christian University Press

Copyright © 2017 by Terry Wardle

ISBN 978-0-89112-493-1 | LCCN 2017014156

Printed in the United States of America

Scripture quotations, unless otherwise noted, are from The Holy Bible, New International Version®, NIV®. Copyright © 1973, 1978, 1984, 2011 by Biblica, Inc.® Used by permission. All rights reserved worldwide.

Scripture quotations noted RSV are taken from the Revised Standard Version of the Bible, copyright © 1946, 1952, and 1971 the Division of Christian Education of the National Council of the Churches of Christ in the United States of America. Used by permission. All rights reserved.

Scripture quotations noted NASB are taken from the New American Standard Bible® Copyright © 1960, 1962, 1963, 1968, 1971, 1972, 1973, 1975, 1977, 1995 by The Lockman Foundation. Used by permission.

LIBRARY OF CONGRESS CATALOGING-IN-PUBLICATION DATA
Names: Wardle, Terry, author.
Title: Identity matters : discovering who you are in Christ / Terry Wardle.
Description: Abilene : Leafwood Publishers, 2017.
Identifiers: LCCN 2017014156 | ISBN 9780891124931 (pbk.)
Subjects: LCSH: Identity (Psychology—Religious aspects—Christianity.
Classification: LCC BV4509.5 .W3724 2017 | DDC 233—dc23
LC record available at https://lccn.loc.gov/201701415 6

Cover design by ThinkPen Design, LLC
Interior text design by Sandy Armstrong, Strong Design

Leafwood Publishers is an imprint of Abilene Christian University Press
ACU Box 29138
Abilene, Texas 79699

1-877-816-4455
www.leafwoodpublishers.com

18 19 20 21 22 / 7 6 5 4 3

To our grandchildren,
here and yet to arrive.

Table of Contents

Chapter One

Identity *Matters*

I remember what happened as though it were yesterday. Even half a century later, I am amazed at how formative the experience was on my sense of self. It accentuated a message I was struggling with, accelerating an already present tendency to believe, if not be convinced, that being me was simply not enough.

I was ten years old and my mother finally allowed me to ride my bike to my grandmother's house about six miles away. When I say "my" bike, that is really only half true. It had been my older sister's bike. A big, blue, girl's Schwinn bike. Bonny now was learning to drive a car, so the bicycle got passed down to me. A big, blue, *girl's* Schwinn bike. It's embarrassing even to write this!

In an attempt to redeem a bit of my masculinity, my step-grandfather drilled a hole at the top of the back fender and attached a pair of saddlebags. He knew I wanted to be a cowboy (in fact, I still do!). The saddlebags were a welcome and needed addition. I found a set of streamers at the five-and-dime to fit into each grip on the handlebars. It was still a big, blue, girl's bike, but these few touches made it mine. I was finally allowed to ride forth on my first great adventure.

I lived in a post-WWII housing development in the small southwestern Pennsylvania town of Finleyville. The housing development, known by everyone in town as the Robert's Plan, was large, and it was spilling over with children my age. I had lots of playmates and we had countless adventures, especially in the woods that bordered the west side of our neighborhood. For some time I had been allowed to ride my bike on the roads near our home. I was not, however, allowed to venture beyond the Robert's Plan.

When I was ten years old, Mom gave in, and I set out on my first long-distance ride . . . alone. I went down the long hill in front of our home, all the way to the main street, Washington Avenue. I turned right and rode the sidewalk about a quarter of a mile, until I turned up the alley by Garry's Funeral Home and hit the back street through Finleyville. I made my way behind the Presbyterian church, past Caprio's Restaurant. Just below Dubb's Market I turned back onto the main street that would lead past the lumberyard on the way toward Rankintown.

I was filled with confidence as I rode out of town, and frankly, I felt older. I had broken free of the constraints of my little neighborhood, and now I was on my own to experience a grand adventure. It was a rite of passage: I was peddling my way past childhood and into adolescence. I felt like a somebody, even on a big, blue, girl's Schwinn bike. With saddlebags!

As I passed the Finleyville Lumberyard at the edge of town, I crossed the railroad tracks and then rumbled over a small creek on a single-lane bridge. The bridge, made of wood and steel, was no big deal. It would take seconds to cross on my bike, a blink of an eye in an automobile. But on that day long ago and yet ever-present to me, it became a bridge too far.

As I began to cross, four teenage boys stepped onto the far side of the bridge. I didn't know them, but, being the brave young man that I was, I intended to smile, maybe say hi, and pass on by. However, they had other things in mind. As I came close to them, one of the boys grabbed my handlebars and spun my bike to an abrupt stop. "Hey, where do you think you're goin'?" he snarled, as another boy chimed in, "Yeah, kid, where ya goin'?"

Instantly I knew they had no interest in the real answer to those questions, but I said anyway, "To my grandmother's." Laughter broke out among them, and they mocked me as only adolescent boys do. One boy knocked me off my bike, and another got on it and started riding it back and forth over the bridge. The fact that it was a big, blue, girl's Schwinn bike did not go unnoticed, even with the saddlebag accessory. It instigated more ridicule, and they piled on the harassment.

I tried to get my bike back, but that only made them dial up the abuse. Soon, one thug grabbed the front of my shirt with his fist and said that they were going to take my bike, but not before they beat me up. I had been told that horses can smell fear. Every horse for two counties around must have had a good whiff of me right then. I was petrified. I couldn't fight or break free to run, so I stood there frozen.

About the time the beating was to begin and my bike was making its way out of sight, one of the bullies asked, "What's your name?" I answered him in a high-pitched preadolescent, quivering voice, "Terry Wardle." The three remaining teenagers got a bit silent and looked at one another nervously. "Are you related to Tom Wardle?"

Tom was a much older cousin, who happened to play defensive end on the high school football team. I knew him, because the Wardle clan was close in our small town. But I had my doubts as to whether Tom knew me.

My three assailants backed off a bit as they waited. I hesitated, trying to come up with the answer that would best preserve my hide. I thought it over and then said, "Yeah, Tom is my brother."

I lied. Straight out, bold-faced, as untrue as any statement I had made to date. But I had high hopes that this lie might be a bodyguard of sorts and get me out of this harassment. And it did.

The three teenagers looked at each other very carefully, then one said to another, "Go get his bike," which set him off on a dead run calling for their fourth thieving friend to come back, and fast.

One of the boys straightened out my shirt, and started saying, "Hey, we were just funning you. No harm. You're a great kid, and . . . if anyone ever gives you any trouble, you tell us and we'll take care of you." Putting my bike back in my hands, they took off running across the bridge the way they came. I stood there, still afraid, alone, shaking all over.

I turned my bike around and headed back through town toward home. I never told my mom or dad what happened. I simply said I changed my mind about going to Grandma's. I was too ashamed to tell them what really took place, and I didn't want them to think I wasn't big enough to venture beyond the Robert's Plan. But it took some time for me to face that journey again, and when I did, I was far less attentive to the passing scenery. My eyes always were looking ahead for any possible trouble coming my way.

That was a formative day for me in more ways than one. I learned, quite existentially, that simply being me was not enough. Being Terry Wardle was not enough to be respected, accepted, and safe. Had I not claimed a connection to Tom Wardle, my bike would have been stolen and I would have been beaten up. It took Tom's name and reputation to get me a bit of respect. I had to attach my existence to his. In the panic of the moment, when the cry for safety was loudest, I lied. Lying was not something I did much. I never handled well the residue of guilt that remained. But in this case, I told a whopper and had no regrets.

That night I was glad to be home safe. I didn't feel like talking to anyone, so I went off to my room to be alone. I was caught in an uncomfortable in-between. On the one hand, everything did turn out okay. My bike was in the garage, and I had no cuts and bruises. On the other hand, I now saw myself as they did, weak and insignificant. I had to pretend to be something I was not or they would have roughed me up. That painful in-between became a familiar landscape for me for decades to come.

Any resolve or decisions I made as a result of that event were more subconscious than conscious. I was a ten-year-old boy then, and my thoughts and perceived needs were primitive at best. But even from the distance of five decades, I see that what occurred that day impacted how I viewed my place in the world. It was one of many such events through childhood, adolescence, and beyond that reinforced not only my perception that this is an unsafe and ungenerous world, but that attaining any degree of success in life would demand much more than simply being me.

Identity Matters

Identity is the foundation on which our individual uniqueness rests. Identity secures that which satisfies the deepest longings of our lives. The ground of our identity, whether rock solid or shifting sand, impacts our self-esteem and self-worth and directly influences the questions of purpose and significance in our quest for meaningful existence. These are by no means small matters. They serve as the structural steel we build our lives on. Identity matters.

Few people spend time thinking deeply about identity, at least in the way I will be considering it here. For most people, any discussion of identity relates more to identity theft, which is ultimately a matter of economics, not philosophy. Because money and identity are so often deeply integrated in our society, many people see them as one and the same, which they most certainly are not.

While I care about the security of my bank accounts, credit cards, and social security number, these digits do not and must not in any way represent who I am as a unique human being. At least, they should not, though current attitudes often reflect the contrary.

Identity integrity must be linked to essential qualities that are secure and eternal. Many followers of Christ, myself included, have been lured away from the realities that in Christ make us unique and significant. We end up identifying with attainments that will, in the long run, spoil and fade, often right before our eyes. Illusive investments are touted in our culture as the gold standard for uniqueness and significance, though they are in fact dead weight that will ultimately bring us down and wear us out.

Identity and the Decisions We Make

How we perceive ourselves, though often subconscious, is a driving force in the most important decisions we will ever make in life. If our identity is founded on what is eternal, then our decisions flow from a deep sense of personal worth and security. On the other hand, if we attach our identity to what the world identifies as necessary to safety and significance, we will live a life that is characterized by performance and exhaustion.

Cathy Tustin[1] came to see me soon after she turned sixty-five years old. The chronic anger she had lived with most of her life had always been toxic. Now she was living on the edge of a debilitating emotional explosion. Cathy knew she had a serious anger problem, but she had not considered that her uncontrollable anger was a secondary response to a much deeper wound that had festered in her for her entire life. It wasn't just any wound. It was an identity wound.

Cathy was the oldest of three siblings, sister to two younger brothers. She was raised in a blue-collar culture with a disengaged father and a controlling mother. Cathy was a bright student who had done well in school. She wanted to go to college, but her mother and father actually put words to a message that had been implicitly present her whole life. "We don't have money to send you to any college. If we did have money, it would be for your brothers. After all, they're boys."

Cathy was determined, even in the face of such gender-demeaning attitudes. She sold the piano her grandmother had willed to her and started to take classes at the local community college. Without encouragement from her parents, Cathy did well. She scraped together enough money to earn an associate degree in accounting. A decent job as a bookkeeper followed, and she excelled at her work.

Relationships, particularly with men, did not come easily for Cathy. While she held her own at work, she struggled with a deep sense of inferiority, more than once getting involved with men who would demean her. After several difficult relationships, she married a man who was better than some she dated. She had two daughters, all the while working and continuing her education.

---

[1]Name changed for anonymity

She advanced in her career, earned a bachelor's degree, and then a master's in business administration.

Lingering beneath the surface of Cathy's life was the identity-wounding attitude of her parents. Boys were more important than girls, and she did not measure up enough for them to invest in her education. Cathy did not speak of this with anyone. The chronic anger increased, however, as the unprocessed wound remained unhealed. The identity insecurity continued to bear bad fruit, emotionally, psychologically, spiritually, and relationally. Cathy could hide the hurt, but inside she was in deep soul pain. Whenever someone accidently touched that wound, some level of acting out resulted. It could get ugly without warning.

Cathy never addressed this pain with her parents. They continued to wound her with their attitude. Even after Cathy advanced to become the CFO of a small manufacturing plant, her parents would introduce her as their daughter, "the bookkeeper." Cathy would tell people she was actually a financial officer, but with her folks, neither the facts of her vocation nor the demeaning attitudes they perpetuated ever sank in.

No matter how successful Cathy became, she never distanced herself from the identity wounding she received from those closest to her. Regardless of how far she advanced educationally, professionally, or financially, Cathy fundamentally believed that she simply did not measure up. No matter what she did, it would never be enough. As a result, she would never be enough.

Cathy Tustin was convinced that deep within she was "less than," and nothing she did would make her "more than." The message her parents imprinted had become her own defining narrative, and it was painful. Cathy needed help from the Holy Spirit to recognize this wounding, to grieve the many losses that had resulted from it, and to meet Jesus in the place of her deepest brokenness. There, and only there, would she discover the true wonder of who she is in Christ: a uniquely gifted child of God lavishly loved by her heavenly Father, regardless of what anyone else on this entire planet believes.

A Dark Strategy

The messages we so often receive in this culture, whether explicitly or implicitly, fundamentally communicate that in ourselves we are not enough. Not enough for what? Not enough to have the deepest longings of our lives met. In other words, as we are, we do not measure up. Because we do not measure up, we lose!

Once this message takes root, it profoundly impacts our self-esteem and self-worth. As a result, we begin—as I did at the bridge—to attach ourselves, through deep personal investments of energy and integrity, to whatever we increasingly believe will make us enough.

This relentless pursuit, characterized by performance and people pleasing, costs us dearly as we try to shape the expectations of those we deem important to our world. These efforts at "self-improvement" fuel a great deal of exhaustion in our lives, as well as discouragement, anxiety, anger, and despair. It leads to increasing investments in strategies of self-promotion motivated by competition and comparison. Instead of seeing the uniqueness in others, we begin to view them in relation to the level of our own identity security. They often become the competition or the standard of our own existence.

It is critical that you see this as a strategy of darkness. It is designed to keep you from ever resting in your true identity as God's dearly loved child. It leads you to be not only judgmental toward yourself, but also to see others through the lenses of suspicion and rejection, rather than enjoying the freedom to love and value each other as the unique children of God that we actually are in Christ Jesus.

Not Everyone Gets It

I sponsor a seminar called Identity Integrity and the Awakening of the True Self. During four days, I try to help people understand the importance of identity integrity and its relationship to the awakening of a person's true self. I am convinced this is a critical matter to well-being. Frankly, not everyone agrees or gets how important this discussion is. Probably Brad[2] said it best.

> Why is this discussion important, anyway? It sounds
> more philosophical than practical. Anyone asks me
> about my identity, I tell them straight. My name is Brad,
> I am the son of Oliver and Nancy, I am Julie's husband,
> and Brian and Carla's dad. I am a math teacher at the
> local high school and have been for eighteen years. I
> make enough money to be comfortable, and we have a
> bit put away for the possible rainy day. I guess I would
> call myself a Christian. At least I go to church once in
> a while, and, compared to most, I am a pretty good guy.
> I could say more, but all said, what's the big deal? I am
> who I am, and that's that.

What Brad said is not without merit. He does seem to have a fairly clear sense of himself, at least at the level of relationships and defining characteristics of his life. To be sure, these are important. But

---

[2]Names changed for anonymity

most of what he lists as identifying marks are qualities he could lose. If the foundation of his identity rests on people and job and roles, life can at times bring difficulties that place each of these at risk. People lose their jobs, and unfortunately even the roles of husband and father, wife and mother. Financial security in our day is also never a sure thing.

What happens to Brad's sense of self if any of the items on his identity inventory are suddenly taken away? If these characteristics are the essence of Brad's identity, who then is he if they are suddenly compromised? I have talked with many people who have placed their identity in people, money, profession, appearance, or even public acclaim. But how secure or eternal are such things? Not at all. When people invest their energy in securing things like these and then lose them, it not only leads to anger and grief; it also brings great identity confusion.

I well remember a discussion with John Reynolds.[3] After forty-five years in pastoral ministry, John retired, looking forward to a new adventure in life with his wife, Carla. However, soon after retirement John began to struggle with mild depression. He told me that even though he could find things to do, he had lost his sense of significance. John said, "For forty-five years I knew who I was. I was Pastor John. That gave me great meaning and purpose. I was a somebody, doing something important every day. Terry, who am I now?"

This hits at the heart of why identity integrity is such a big deal. It is the foundation of your uniqueness, the source of satisfaction of the deepest longings of your life. By "foundation," I mean it is the underlying strength, or weakness, that upholds the meaning

---

[3] Names changed for anonymity

and significance of your existence. Identity is not what you do, nor is it about what you have, and it is definitely not about how others see you. Those characteristics are not ultimately unimportant. They are characteristics of your life, but identity itself goes much deeper.

When you build uniqueness on characteristics and qualities that have in themselves an essential insecurity, then your identity will always be at risk. This book is a discussion not only of why identity matters, but also of how critical it is that the foundation of your identity be secure and eternal.

While I will explore this in detail in the chapters to come, it is enough here to say that the secure and eternal foundation is in Christ alone, identified best by these few words: "I am a child of God." Not I am a pastor, teacher, husband, father, or friend. It is not I am a celebrity, wealthy, athletic, strong, or weak. The foundation of identity for a Christian must be this, and only this: "I am a child of God." That is the identifying mark of a secure life. That is the single characteristic that will bring you ultimate satisfaction and significance. Everything else, such as being a pastor, husband, son, daughter, math teacher, or doctor, rests on that reality. And, because of Christ, your identity is not only secure, it is eternal.

For Your Reflection

1. Ask the Holy Spirit to help you review the incidents of your life. Did you ever experience a personal "bridge too far"?

2. What messages did that send you?

3. Did you ever sense that in yourself you were not enough? What impact did that have on you emotionally?

4. How did you respond?

5. In what ways have you worked to measure up to the expectations of others?

6. Identity is the foundation of a person's uniqueness. What does that concept mean to you?

7. Why is it important that you not build your identity on things such as job, finances, appearance, and relationships?

8. What does it mean that your identity is "child of God"? What difference does that make?

9. What do you sense the Lord saying to you regarding the discussion in the chapter?

Chapter Two

How Firm Is Your *Foundation*?

When I was fifteen I began to work for Tommy McCoy's construction company, and I continued to do so during summers and on weekends until I was twenty-five. Tommy ran a crew that built homes in the suburbs of Pittsburgh, Pennsylvania. Initially, I started as a carpenter's helper, but in time I learned the skills of a carpenter and ran a framing crew on several jobs. I loved the work, and to this day I get deep satisfaction from any task that involves power saws, wood, hammers, and nails.

Tommy McCoy built new homes contracted by owners. They would pick out the plans, the building lot, and visit the construction site countless times, beginning with plotting out the layout of the home on the ground, all the way to the moment when we handed them the key when we were done.

I was involved in numerous conversations with owners. They would ask questions, give directives, and more often than not evaluate how they thought we were doing. They also (quite regularly I might add) changed their minds. This meant something had to be undone so that something different could be constructed in its place. That could involve literally anything, from placement of walls, style of windows, location of plumbing and electrical installations, to simple things like the color of paint.

In all these owner/contractor conversations I observed and participated in, there was one matter I never heard much discussion about. Yet it was the most important part of building a house—the foundation. The owners could go on and on about the size of rooms, texture of the plaster, types of kitchen cabinets, color of shingles on the roof, and even the landscaping. But they seldom mentioned the foundation.

I have overheard owners dream about placement of furniture, what the kids' rooms would look like, where to use carpet or hardwood flooring, and the style and colors of the window treatments. This makes sense to some degree because that is where life will take place for them. These things contribute to the quality of life they will live in this home. This is where love will be shown, friends will gather, naps will be taken, and decisions made. It is little wonder that planning these matters is important.

Foundations of homes are not attractive. In fact, most people never see them. A foundation is built deep beneath the frost line where a footer is laid to support the cement blocks upon which the house is built.. The foundation is concrete, which is cold, gray, unattractive, and mostly hidden beneath the ground.

Owners usually ask few questions about the foundation, seldom if ever take visitors to see the foundation, and certainly can't wait until the builders get past fooling with the foundation so the house, where real life takes place, can be built and eventually enjoyed.

While all this is true, no part of the home is more important than its foundation. Compromise there and everything else is at risk. Ignore the specifications for depth, width, and strength of the foundation and sooner rather than later everything above it gets thrown off plumb, and the ultimate security and value of the home quickly declines. The foundation may be ignored and unseen by most, but its importance will never be questioned by a responsible builder.

Identity is the foundation of the life we live, but the majority of people, at least those I know and interact with, do not think much about identity. Why? I guess it is because they are too busy being attentive to the demands of life itself. Just as a homeowner gives a great deal of attention to what makes a home welcoming and comfortable, people are intent upon dealing with what they see to be the important aspects of life. They invest in family, friends, jobs, finances, and all the other matters that consume our days, weeks, months, and years.

However, just as it is with a home, all of what makes up your life is built on the foundation of identity. Regardless of whether you spend time seriously considering what your life is founded on, it still matters, and it matters greatly. The security of your identity directly impacts how you perceive yourself, build relationships, respond to the circumstances of daily life, engage at the workplace, and react to criticism or rejection.

Where you place your identity is the foundation of personal well-being, whether that is the quality of your physical, psychological, or emotional health. It also profoundly impacts spiritual matters, including how you pursue Christian maturity, the level of security you have as a believer, the ways you engage and resist the strategies of evil, and how you perceive the admonition of Scripture to walk in practical holiness.

Where you place your identity determines the difference between dancing to the tune the world plays, hiding parts of yourself to gain acceptance and significance from an ever-judgmental world, or being secure enough to say yes to God's invitation to allow your true self to emerge as the chosen, beloved, and empowered child of God you are. Once you understand who you are in Christ—a loved child of God—you will be able to stand against the constant messages the world throws your way and enter the rest that comes to all who are confident of the Father's eternal acceptance and love.

Howard Thurman

Howard Thurman was born in Florida in 1899, and lived in Waycross, one of Daytona's black communities. Faith was a foundational pillar of his life, influenced by his mother, Alice, and his maternal grandmother and former slave, Nancy Ambrose, who took him faithfully to Mount Bethel Baptist Church in Waycross.

Thurman was a brilliant young man, eventually graduating from Morehouse College and what is now Colgate Rochester Crozier Divinity School, in both cases as valedictorian. Howard Thurman went on to serve as pastor, philosopher, educator, and civil rights leader. He was respected as one of the most important figures, not only in African American history, but in American history as well. His influence on Martin Luther King, among countless others, is well documented.

Howard Thurman wrote over twenty books, several celebrated as required reading at countless institutions across the globe. His writing has certainly influenced my own thinking, not least in the area of identity integrity and Christian values. For almost twenty years, I have required all my doctoral students to read his classic work *Jesus and the Disinherited,* a profound treatment of the evil of racism and marginalization and of the need for people everywhere to find their true identity in God alone. Howard Thurman writes:

> The awareness of being a child of God tends to stabilize the ego and results in new courage, fearlessness, and power. I have seen it happen again and again.
>
> When I was a youngster, this was drilled into me by my grandmother. The idea was given to her by a certain slave minister who, on occasion, held secret religious meetings with his fellow slaves. How everything in me quivered with the pulsing terror of raw energy, when, in her recital, she would come to the triumphant climax of the minister. "You—you are not n-----s. You—you are not slaves. You are God's children!" This established for them the ground of personal dignity, so that a profound sense of personal worth could absorb the fear reaction. . . . This individual now feels that he counts, that he belongs. He senses the confirmation of his roots, and even death becomes a little thing.[1]

We must not forget that the focal point of Dr. Thurman's critique is those disinherited by society, declared to be less than and unworthy of equal treatment and respect under the law. Thurman is seeking to infuse understanding regarding the plight of the marginalized and to impart hope to those who have been pushed to the back of this society's bus. I would never want, nor intend, to minimize the horrendous and unjust discrimination some have suffered by suggesting that we can all relate to Thurman's descriptions of the disrespected.

I do believe, however, that we can learn much from Thurman's warnings about allowing a broken world controlled by darkness to determine our value and importance as human beings. Even those who would undoubtedly be categorized as the privileged have been undermined at the foundation of their lives. Evil has tried to drive all of us to seek security and significance through striving and performance, all the while reminding us in countless ways that on our own we simply do not measure up. Unfortunately, plagued by the disease of comparison and competition, many take sick solace in the thought that some folks measure up even less than they do.

While embracing the call to champion social reform and social justice for all, Howard Thurman knew that in the final analysis a person must find the strength and significance of his or her life in what God and God alone declares to be true.

> The core of the analysis of Jesus is that man is a child of God, the God of life that sustains all of nature and guarantees all the intricacies of the life process itself. Jesus suggests that it is quite unreasonable to assume that God, whose creative activity is expressed even in such details as the hairs of a man's head, would exclude from his concern the life, the vital spirit, of the man himself. [2]

Howard Thurman believed that the truth of one's identity in Christ must be repeatedly declared to all people. It is the only way that men and women might reject the disqualifying and demeaning messages so often vocalized in this world and rise up to allow the wonder of individual uniqueness to emerge in full view. He said:

> There is something more to be said about the inner equipment growing out of the great affirmation of Jesus that a man is a child of God. If a man's ego has been stabilized, resulting in a sure grounding of his sense of personal worth and dignity, then he is in position to appraise his own intrinsic powers, gifts, talents, and abilities.[3]

I love that phrase, "sure grounding." When a person's identity rests on sure grounding, he or she is able to resist the strategies of this world to beat people down as a way to get them to measure up. Instead, the child of God is able through Christ to sense his or her own worth and dignity and to allow the true self to awaken in strength and glory. Jesus crossed a universe to secure this for all of us. If we could rest in what is true of us in Christ, we would see through the efforts of a darkened world to blind us to how Jesus really sees us and desires that we see ourselves.

Dan McKinnon is a dear friend. He is a Canadian pastor who serves in Ottawa, and, most importantly, he is a Kingdom man. He gets it and spends his life helping people do the same. I am gifted not only to know Dan as friend and a coworker for the Lord, but to be the object of his constant prayers before the throne.

Recently, Dan emailed these words to me, written by James Hudson Taylor in his work *Union and Communion*. Taylor wrote, "Well it is when our eyes are filled with His beauty and our hearts are occupied with Him. In the measure in which this is true of us we shall recognize the correlative truth that His great heart is occupied with us."[4]

The richness of these words must penetrate our hearts. God cares about us, loves us, thinks about us, which should serve to reinforce our worth and significance, graced to us through Christ. We are children of God, held in his heart for all eternity. Knowing this should steel us deep within and ground our identity in the secure and eternal designation "child of God." This should fill our minds with possibilities and, as Howard Thurman said, cause our "hearts to whisper, 'Thank you and Thank God!'"[5]

Three Stories

The life we live, with all its decisions and responses, reflects our understanding of who we truly are. This is true now and has been true throughout the centuries. Scripture bears witness to this truth. I will here cite three stories that show us in part what a difference identity integrity makes.

Judges 6:11–16

Most Christians have heard of Gideon and his courageous victory over the Midianite and Amalekite armies, numbering in the tens of thousands. What makes this victory especially amazing is the fact that God whittled down Gideon's army from thirty-two thousand to a mere three hundred men. It took courage and sheer obedience for Gideon and his men to move into battle against a horde of enemies. In faithfulness, this is precisely what they did. God rewarded their faith and gave them a mighty victory. Gideon received a place in the faith hall of fame recorded in Hebrews 11.

But this grand story of faith and courage certainly did not begin that way. Gideon started off deathly afraid of the Midianites. So much so that he was threshing his wheat in a winepress to avoid being seen by the marauders. God sent an angel to Gideon and greeted him with the words, "The Lord is with you, mighty warrior." Gideon certainly did not see himself that way, even describing himself to the angel as from the "weakest clan in Manasseh, and I am the least in my family."

Gideon saw himself as a weak nothing, and yet the Lord saw him in his true identity. He was a child of God and, as such, God was with him. Gideon questioned God's intentions, and yet the Lord said, "Go in the strength you have and save Israel." What did God see that no one else did? What strength was he talking about, given that Gideon was hiding in a winepress and self-identifying as weak and insignificant?

The Lord clarified by asking Gideon a question, "Am I not sending you?" Why is this significant? Because it was God's statement of Gideon's identity. He was God's man, a part of God's chosen people, and therefore equipped to do anything and everything God asked of him. He was not weak and insignificant. God himself formed Gideon, just as he has formed you and me. Gideon had forgotten this fact and hid in a winepress. God called him to rise up into his true self. Ever since, the name of Gideon has been held in esteem and respect.

1 Samuel 15:1–35

The Israelites clamored for a king. So, through Samuel the priest, God anointed Saul to rule over them. The Scriptures say that Saul stood tall among his peers and was honored by the people. Samuel had made it clear, however, that Saul was to be obedient to God in all ways and, if he was, blessings would follow his reign.

Saul was under specific instructions from the Lord to go up against the armies of the Amalekites. But Saul failed to follow those commands, choosing instead to make his own decisions regarding the battle. This displeased the Lord, and he sent Samuel to communicate this to Saul. King Saul tried to justify his actions, but one sentence holds the key to understanding Saul's disobedience. He said, "I was afraid of the men so I gave in to them."

This action speaks volumes about identity insecurity. When a person, like Saul or any of us, needs the approval of others to such a degree that we would compromise what we know to be best, that action reveals that our identity does not rest secure with God. While not one of us takes pleasure in being rejected or even attacked, being driven by the will of others is a sign that our identity and the corresponding issues of security and significance are in the hands of other people, not God. To say the least, this is a sign that things need to change with our understanding of who we are in Christ.

2 Samuel 19:22-23

David, King of Israel, faced an ugly time in his reign. His son Absalom rose up against him, declared himself to be king, and sent David fleeing for his life. Shimei of Gera stood by the road and insulted David in vile, abusive terms. David's companions wanted David to strike down the loudmouth, but David saw no need. He was seeking to find where the Lord was in these events, even in Shimei's words (2 Sam. 16:10–12).

Later, after Absalom was defeated and David was returning to Jerusalem, Shimei fell before the king and asked for forgiveness. David's men wanted him put to death for cursing David, the Lord's anointed. David had the power to do this, and by all accounts he had the right. But his response was profound in its maturity. David said, "Don't I know that today I am king over Israel?" He then forgave Shimei and assured him that he would not die that day.

This is the epitome of identity integrity and security. David knew who he was in God's eyes, and neither difficult circumstances nor disrespect changed this in David's heart. He entrusted himself to God and to God's care. Disrespect and verbal abuse from others such as Shimei did not shatter David's sense of significance or security before the Lord. He was able to respond to life's challenges rather than allowing fear to drive him to disbelieve what God had already declared to be true. That is the power of identity security.

Too often I have identified myself as weak and insignificant, and then worked hard to convince myself and others that this was not true. When I did accomplish something acceptable and impressive, I told myself that the achievement would solidify my significance. I have also, like Saul, worried about what others thought of me and therefore compromised what I knew to be God's will for my life. I have allowed myself to believe the message of insignificance peddled by the world rather than to stand on the solid rock of who I am in Christ.

These are some of the key reasons why understanding the critical issue of identity is essential for personal well-being. Rather than exhausting ourselves in a relentless pursuit of security and significance, which the world always holds back regardless of accomplishment, we need to discover the wonder of who we are in Christ and stand there and only there, on the firm foundation that is ours as children of God.

What Difference Does This Make, Really?

We must move beyond the theological and philosophical dimensions of identity and consider practical reasons why we should pay attention to the foundation of our significance and security. One way to do that is through a series of questions that highlight the different dimensions of this discussion.

Self-Definition

The first question is straightforward and direct: Is your identity resting on what is constant and unchangeable, or is it easily compromised by the actions of others?

The Scriptures say that nothing "will be able to separate us from the love of God that is in Christ Jesus" (Rom. 8:39). Those important words follow a lengthy discussion by Paul of what it means to be a child of God. The bottom line of that discussion is the revelation that we belong to him and, as his children, neither hell nor high water will shake us off that foundation. That is identity security.

On the other hand, do you find that circumstances, including the attitudes of others, bring fear to you and shatter your sense of significance? I remember well when I was placed on the crew run by Tommy McCoy's brother. I went there feeling pretty good about myself. That did not last long. John was brutal with me. He demeaned me at every turn, screamed all the time, and made fun of me in front of others. His actions shook my confidence and, as a result, the quality of my work.

This went on for weeks. I began to have trouble sleeping, wondered what I could do to get him to like me, and thought seriously about quitting. One day, in the midst of a tirade witnessed by other workers, John said, "Your ol' man threw rotten eggs at me when I was just a kid. You Wardles are all a--holes as far as I am concerned." At one level I now understood what was driving his abuse. But on the other hand, I was sick inside and wanted to hide in a hole in the ground. I went from feeling good about myself to terrible.

What had changed? In Christ, nothing. I was still a child of God and secure in him. But I had allowed someone else to define me, and that was a huge mistake. We all must learn that no one gets to define us but Jesus.

Self-Worth

The next question: What is your attitude toward yourself? Do you see yourself as a person of dignity and worthy of respect? You should. Granted, we are broken people and have more than a few issues that need to be addressed by the transforming work of the Holy Spirit. Yet God's love sent Jesus to our world, where he spilled his blood to bring us into the embrace of our Father. Do you understand that the Holy Spirit has enabled you to share the nature of Christ now that you believe, and as a result you are his work of art regardless of the garbage yet to be cleansed from your life? Children of God, such as you are, are lavished with his love (1 John 3:1), and that identity instills in you dignity that you and others are to respect.

When our identity is not secure in Christ, not founded on what is eternal, circumstances can easily cause us to experience inadequacy and feel shame toward ourselves. How well I remember a school basketball game I was playing in. My coach was an ex-Marine maniac who believed fear was the best motivation for good athleticism. Man, was he wrong. In a game my parents came to watch, I lost the ball on one play and then tossed up an airball on the next.

Coach Chaos (my name for him) yanked me off the court, practically ripping my game shirt right off my back. In front of fans and family he screamed at me with spit flying, and shouted for me to get to the end of the bench. Rather than concluding that he was acting like an abusive idiot, I turned on myself. I took up where he let off and felt embarrassed to be me.

Wow, how insecure is that, to allow someone else not only to define me, but to agree with his judgment? I wish that was the last time something like that happened to me, but in truth, I often have allowed the acceptance and evaluation of others to determine whether I feel good about myself. Do you identify with this? If so, possibly you, like me, need to allow the Lord (and nothing or no one else) to determine your worth.

Sense of Acceptance

Question number three: What determines your sense of belonging? Belonging to a community—being accepted by others—is one of the fundamental longings of our lives. Not only do we naturally desire to belong, when the community we belong to is healthy, we actually function better at almost every level. God, who exists as Three in One, has created us to be connected with him and with one another.

My paternal grandfather divorced my grandmother before they had been married four years. My father and his sister were young children, so, looking for someone to care for them, my grandfather married again, this time to an Eastern European lady named Matilda. She was the best grandmother a kid could ever want.

There was a time, though, when Eastern Europeans were not held in high esteem in our small town. In fact, they were discriminated against regularly. When Grandma's sister and brother-in-law went to the bank after saving enough down payment money to secure a loan for a home, the discrimination they encountered was blatant.

Danny McDaniels was the bank president in our town back then, and he looked down on Eastern Europeans. He was willing to provide a home loan only if that home was on the wrong side of the tracks. They had the money for a much nicer home, but he would not budge. In his mind, they were across-the-tracks kind of people, and across the tracks they would stay. For as long as I knew them, this stigma affected their sense of belonging. They were only second-class people, and they just had to make peace with that.

First John 4:15–16 is a beautiful text that reads, "If anyone acknowledges that Jesus is the Son of God, God lives in them and they in God. And so we know and rely on the love God has for us." That acceptance and belonging are both secure and eternal. When you place your identity in Christ, you belong to him, and, according to this Scripture, you belong to God. You never have to earn that acceptance, and because of Jesus you will never lose it. You are a cherished part of the family of God, a citizen of the Kingdom, and part of the greatest story in the universe.

It never feels good to have people exclude you, regardless of the reason. It is okay to say that it hurts. But the rejection of others is never—not once, not ever—a statement about your place in the heart of God. You need not work at pleasing or performing to gain entry into his eternal family. You are his child, you belong to him eternally, and that truth will hold you fast whenever others do not see or will not accept the wonder of who you are.

The Satisfaction of Your Deepest Longings

We all have core desires that are soul deep and that motivate a lot of our behaviors and responses in life. We previously mentioned significance, safety, and belonging. Add to those love, purpose, and understanding, and you have a fistful of core longings that must never be taken lightly. The question then is, "How are these deepest longings satisfied?"

On multiple occasions each year, in seminars, classes, and conversations, I ask several basic questions related to core longings. Invariably, the first is, "Where does the world encourage you to place your significance?" Answers come quickly and often with much energy. "Money. Job. Family. Degrees. Appearance. Titles." I usually follow that question with similar ones about acceptance, security, purpose, and even love. The answers do not change.

The world would encourage you to expend great amounts of time and energy trying to prove that you measure up. Performance as a pathway to identity is an exhausting strategy that only temporarily, at best, provides some satisfaction to our deepest longings.

God's plan for core longings is not performance, but inheritance. In Galatians, Paul wrote that Jesus came, born of a woman, in order than we might be called the children of God. He went on to state that God has provided his children with an inheritance. Unlike inheritances in our culture, the child of God does not need to wait until someone dies to lay claim. As recorded in 1 John 3:1, "See what great love the Father has lavished on us, that we should be called children of God! And that is what we are!"

You are God's child, which means that you are significant. You are loved, accepted, and secure. He has given you purpose, and he understands and delights in your uniqueness. All of your core longings are met in him, because you are his child. You need not perform or strive, or earn, or plead for anything. Your identity is "child of God," and all these blessings follow. That is the grace and generosity of God toward his beloved children.

How You Approach God

One more question: How do you view your interaction with God? There are more than a few Christians who have what I call a transactional approach to God. In a transaction, one party has something you want, and you have something they want. It's that simple. You must give in order to receive. We have a soda machine at the seminary, and it takes a transaction to get the soft drink you desire. The machine wants six quarters, and you want a soda. You give what the machine requires, and the machine gives you the drink you want. Transaction.

That is an insecure foundation upon which to approach God, yet many people see Christianity in those terms. God, in their view, has countless blessings that they greatly desire. However, God requires obedience and holiness, and, as they understand it, he dispenses blessings in exchange for good conduct and sin management. To some degree, although far more sophisticated in its development, it is like the Santa Claus tactic of watching to see who is naughty or nice. Transactions then solicit good gifts or coal!

This approach to God is undeniably popular and unquestionably insecure. Christ Jesus has, through his life and death, drawn you into a relationship with God. You are his child, he is your Father. Any and all requirements you might consider offering are worthless in light of what Jesus has done for you. As Paul said in 2 Corinthians 1:20, the promises of God are yours through Christ Jesus. Does he love you? Yes, because of Christ. Will he watch over you? Absolutely, because of Christ. Are your sins forgiven? Completely. Why? Again, because of Jesus.

I could go on and on, but the answer will be the same. The foundation of your relationship with God is not your performance, but his. Child of God is your identity, and resting secure in it will awaken you to the wonder of your true self, hidden forever in the eternal light of Christ Jesus

For Your Reflection

1. Where did you sense the Holy Spirit speaking to you as you read this chapter? What was he saying?

2. Where have you placed the foundation of your uniqueness?

3. Why is looking at this important to you?

4. Why do you think most people do not spend time carefully considering the issues of identity? Why should they?

5. What were the most important lessons for you out of the stories of Gideon, Saul, and David?

6. What difference does identity make on the following?

Self-definition

Self-worth

Sense of acceptance

Core longings

Relationship with God

7. What best characterizes your approach to God? Transaction or relationship?

Notes

[1] Howard Thurman, *Jesus and the Disinherited* (New York: Abingdon Press, 1949; Boston: Beacon Press, 1976), 50. Citations refer to the Beacon edition. I decided to not write out the derogatory words found in the original text.

[2] Ibid, 49. It should be noted that Howard Thurman wrote this book before we, as a society, were attentive to the issues of gender-inclusive language. While certainly his heart was for all people, regardless of gender, race, religion, or class, his writing, like all good English of his generation, addresses humanity in the masculine "man" and does not reflect a style we embrace today.

[3] Ibid., 53.

[4] James Hudson Taylor, *Union and Communion or Thoughts on the Song of Solomon.* (Lexington, KY: privately printed, 1894), 9.

[5] Thurman, *Jesus and the Disinherited*, 112.

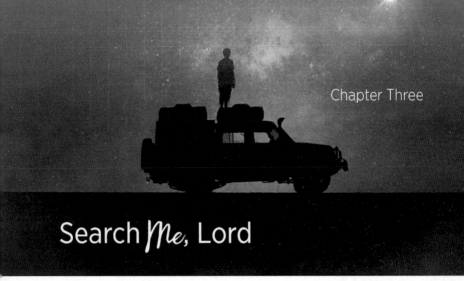

Search *Me*, Lord

I am going to share a personal story to highlight my weakness and insecurity. It would be easy to conclude that I am pointing my finger at the inappropriate actions of others. That is not my purpose. I desire to show how identity insecurity impacts a person's ability to respond to opposition maturely and confidently. Unfortunately, this was not how it worked for me, which I regret.

Thirty years ago, when I was a much younger man, I was appointed to a leadership position with an international Christian organization. This was an extremely important, and for some, coveted post. I was hired to lead an educational institution with responsibilities as the chief executive officer.

This appointment came unexpectedly, but it did impact my sense of acceptance and significance. I approached this responsibility as a call from the Lord, and said yes because I wanted to be faithful in service to the Kingdom. But it is true, a part of this simply made me feel better about myself. I was elevated to a position of great importance, my wife and family were quite proud of me, and I gained entry to a circle of leaders previously closed to me.

The people who were immediately affected by this decision—educators, students, and administrative personnel—could not have been more encouraging. While the choice was as much a surprise to them as it was to me, they were in my corner and ready to dig in and help. That was an indescribable gift to me, motivation to give everything I had to serve effectively as a servant of Christ.

A few factors did call my appointment into question, but initial considerations were that the broader community would be patient with those and bless my selection. In some cases this was true. But a vocal and strong group within the international family began not only to question my selection, but to oppose it quite vigorously.

In some cases I was able to meet with folks, hear their concerns, and calm some of their fears. I grew from the experience. Objections seemed to revolve around three issues. I was much younger than anyone else in the nation holding such a position of leadership. I was quite new to this family of believers, so they did not know me, nor had I earned their confidence. Third, I held a different theological position on a few matters traditionally honored within this group.

All three of these concerns were legitimate, and from a perspective of thirty years later, I question my selection as much as they did those many years ago. However, at that time, questioning these issues brought out my own insecurity, and I was looking forward to the whole thing passing.

Unfortunately, it did not pass. One particular group of leaders began a campaign, questioning my qualifications for this post and raising concerns about who I was as a person. A letter-writing campaign began. Missives sent to the sponsoring body's board of directors demanded that I be replaced. This happened without any face-to-face conversations with me by those who were most upset. This conflict began to affect not only my mood, but also my confidence. Some on the board felt "led" to send me copies of the most inflammatory letters, which included phrases like:

> "Terry Wardle is like a piece of apple pie covered with dead flies . . . "

> "I will rejoice when I see his ministry in ashes."

> "People like him eventually abandon the faith, or become psychopaths."

These comments came from leaders who applied pressure to see me removed. For sure, these folks crossed a line. Their concerns about my age, my tenure, and my theology were legitimate. But their strategy, not so much.

Now to the point. Even though plenty of people were supportive, and encouraging me not to take these attacks seriously, I was deeply hurt. I tried not to show it, but the impact of the opponents' words went deep.

Over and over again I found myself rehearsing hurtful words. I was angry and trying to hide it. My true feelings did leak out, especially around my family. It bothered me that in my less-than-objective opinion, key people did not come to my defense. This storm went on inside me entirely too long, eventually contributing to my decision to leave that position after two years. I moved across the country, hoping that geographic distance would help.

Distance did not help, nor did time. For quite awhile, little things would trigger repressed feelings. Almost any level of criticism became a serious problem. Be clear at this point. The real problem was not found in what was taking place with other people. This was an identity issue. I did not have enough emotional security or confidence in who I was to stay the course, trust God and his purposes, and weather the storm. I allowed those ugly comments to be another evaluation that I simply did not measure up. Just being me was still not enough, and the insecurity of my identity, obviously founded upon my own performance, left me wanting and wounded.

What was the solution? Obviously I needed to forgive these brothers who had allowed their own brokenness to motivate some less than good choices. But what was the path to my freedom? How could I keep from being baited to question my own sense of worth?

My solution certainly was not to try harder, to up my game, to confront those who opposed me, or to run to another job. I needed to go on a journey of descent, deep within my own soul. The words of the psalmist, "Search me, O Lord," had to become the deepest cry of my heart. I had to allow the Holy Spirit to deal with wounds, and loss, and false beliefs I had been holding. I needed to discover that my security rests solidly and solely on this one truth: I am a child of God.

A Journey of Descent

There is a difference between securing your identity on the foundation of being a child of God, versus the constant pressure to prove that you are more than the world says you are. Understanding what being a child of God means is a huge first step toward the awakening of the true self. Yet you must move beyond understanding to actually living out of that identity. That will not happen by applying the same strategy you have been using: namely, performance.

More than a few Christians have been taught that God wants them to be more than they are. They have come to believe they must, through herculean effort, work to ascend to the high ground of Christian maturity. It is as if there is a standard of spirituality existing far above, and through striving, self-improvement, and sin management, they might attain the heights where the Lord dispenses blessings to the worthy. So they work hard and perform, trying to secure their identity as God's child.

Identity integrity does not work that way. It is not a matter of understanding the basics of true Christian identity conceptually and then working hard at ascending to the new and better ground through performance and effort. It demands a willingness on our part to make a journey of descent. We must allow the Holy Spirit to move into the places of our own brokenness and desolation. There the Spirit will ask us to join him in cleansing the garbage of wounds, loss, and false beliefs that has driven our dysfunctional strategies of self-improvement.

The accumulated debris of unprocessed and unhealed wounding, as well as dysfunctional behaviors, keeps Christians from resting securely in their identity in Christ. Knowing about identity security is a great first step, but Spirit-empowered transformation and healing must take place to clear away the garbage so that a person's true self can thrive on the foundation of being a child of God. This demands a journey of descent, not striving or performance.

Anselm Gruen is a Benedictine Father who resides at the Abbey of Munsterschwarzach in Germany. He is the author of three hundred books, one of them a favorite of mine. In it he speaks of this journey of descent:

> The paradox to our spiritual path consists in the fact
> that we ascend to God by descending into our own real-
> ity. . . . By descending into our earth-boundness (humil-
> ity is derived from humus, or soil) we come into contact
> with heaven, with God. When we find the courage to
> climb down into our passions, they lead us to God.[1]

Gruen moves on to explain the nature of that journey of descent,
referring to it as spirituality from below.

> Spirituality from below points out that we come to God
> through careful self-observation and sincere self-knowl-
> edge. We don't find out what God wants from us in the
> lofty ideals we set for ourselves. Often these are merely
> the expression of our ambition. We wish to achieve
> high ideals to look better in the eyes of others and God.
> Spirituality from below thinks that we can discover
> God's will for us, that we can find our vocation, only
> if we have the courage to descend into our own reality
> and deal with our passions, our drives, our needs and
> wishes. The way to God leads through our weaknesses
> and powerlessness.[2]

Three phrases are worthy of attention in Gruen's description: "careful self-observation, sincere self-knowledge, courage to descend."
In simpler terms, the journey of descent demands a long hard look
at the patterns of our lives, and then a courageous willingness
to go beneath those patterns to see what garbage is keeping us
from freedom.

I had to chuckle when I first read Gruen's admonition regarding having the courage to descend. It sent me back over thirty-five

years to the first church I pastored. It was in a small village called Amity, a place with a few houses, a fire department, one store, two churches, and a post office. The people there were mostly farmers and factory workers, and they loved to brag about the benefits of country living.

We had two water sources for the home the church provided. There was an old well and an even older cistern. I wasn't familiar with cisterns, but I soon learned that it was definitely a mixed blessing. Our cistern captured rainwater that ran off our roof. Everyone bragged that cistern water left your clothes soft after washing. Great. But we did notice that while they may have been soft, they also came out of the wash a bit grimy.

We told the trustees of the church about the problem and they said the solution was rather simple. "Just take off the concrete lid, pump out the water, climb down into the concrete tank, and clean it out." That was no small deal. It took three men to remove the concrete lid, and quite a while to pump out the water. It was then and only then that I realized how bad this process was going to be.

I had to climb down into the tank, stand in a foot of sludge and mud, and haul it up the ladder bucket by bucket. I peered into that dark mess quite a while before I worked up the courage to descend! Once I did, I was covered with muck and found dead critters in the mud, not the least of which were rats. To these folks, this was all part of the charm of country living. For me, this was claustrophobic torture in darkness I hoped to never repeat. However, they were right. That water did clean our clothes and make them soft.

Most people want the source of their problems to come from the outside, and they hope the solution is the same. But the most important work that sets us free to live lives based on our identity in

Christ takes place deep inside our own souls. That is why our Lord admonished us to "clean the inside of the cup" (Matt. 23:25–28).

We move into the security of identity integrity by first passing through the darkness of our own wounds, loss, and false beliefs. That does not sound easy, and it is not. Few of us find the idea exciting, and most of us would rather keep all this mess in the dark. Unfortunately, the debris does not remain in the past; it impacts us every day in both subtle and not so subtle ways.

It takes time and patience to make this journey. Led by the Holy Spirit, we will experience healing and cleansing. The garbage of the world's values and our dysfunctional choices will be cleared away, enabling us to stand secure as the children of God we are.

Embracing the Journey

Anselm Gruen, as noted previously, said that the only way to ascend to God is to first descend into ourselves. With that in mind, I have created a V diagram that illustrates the nature of that journey. You will notice that the movement toward freedom and security begins on a downward path. You move beneath the surface of your responses and reactions in life, seeking to discover what holds you in bondage. When you see the power that the past has, you can reach the point of surrender. That is when you are able to move closer toward your ever-awakening true self.

Three truths are worth noting even before the journey begins. To begin with, the only way to ascend is to descend. First the desolation, then the consolation. You must not run and hide from the darkness of your past. Doing so only leaves important parts of your story, parts of yourself, locked away where hope remains unborn. In the Lord's way, and in his timing, you are encouraged to go beneath the surface and see what festers unhealed within.

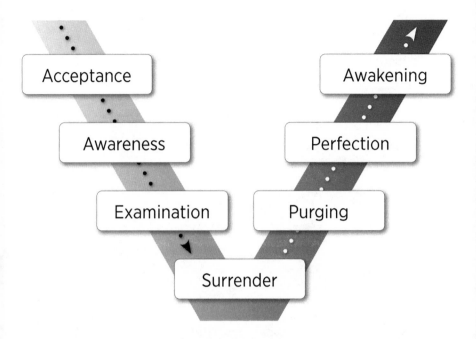

Second, you cannot move horizontally. There are those who give the impression that a horizontal move is possible. They encourage people to forget the past, lay claim to the promises of God, and move into the future. That sounds good, but it never works. Why? Because by moving horizontally, you never deal with the deepest issues that compromise your well-being. Efforts to bypass the deep inner darkness leave problems there to keep you in bondage to the values of this world. You must, with the present help of the Holy Spirit, journey into the depths of your own brokenness if you hope to walk in the freedom that is yours as a child of God.

Third, this is not a one-time journey. You will visit these stages again and again. I am not saying that you will keep working on the same issue again and again. You will revisit each stage. Why? Because the Lord does not deal with every deep loss, lie, and wound of your life at one time. He chooses the issue and moves you through it toward freedom. You can be moving toward freedom in one issue, while others are yet to be revealed.

There will be times when you do revisit something from the past more than once. This happens so the Lord can take you even deeper on your journey of healing. At times, you are healed at the level of your understanding, only to later see the same issue from an even deeper perspective. This is the ever-evolving nature of the journey.

Unprocessed loss, lies, and wounds of the past must be faced. This is the way of freedom, and with freedom comes the ability to build your life on the secure and eternal identity, child of God. The next chapter will further define what it means to say yes to this transforming journey.

For Your Reflection

1. What feelings arose as you read this chapter, and why?

2. Did you find yourself experiencing resistance or dissonance as you read, and if so, why?

3. What did Gruen mean when he said that "we ascend to God by descending into our own reality"?

4. Why does this take courage?

5. What is the importance of "careful self-observation and sincere self-knowledge" as each relates to this journey?

6. What does it mean, "We move into the security of identity integrity by first passing through the darkness of our own wounds, loss, and lies"?

7. Why is it essential that the Holy Spirit lead this journey?

8. What do you sense the Lord asking of you related to this discussion?

9. How would you describe the cistern metaphor to others?

Notes

[1] Anselm Gruen, *Heaven Begins Within You: Wisdom from the Desert Fathers* (New York: Crossroad, 1999), 21.

[2] Ibid., 24.

Chapter Four

Going *Deeper*

When you are embracing this journey, you will see more than a few places where brokenness, weakness, and sinfulness have become debris in your soul. Seeing those things and feeling the pain of hurts and wounds can cause anyone to back up and say no to the journey. It can cause you to experience more than a little self-contempt and self-rejection. That attitude is a giant barrier and never leads to freedom. It is one thing to desire freedom and choose repentance. It is another thing to choose self-hatred and self-judgment. Those postures lead to more bondage, not to freedom and identity security.

Self-hatred and similar attitudes create more desolation, not less. There is a healthy regret in repentance. We all wish we had chosen better and acted more in line with Christ, and we wish that certain things never happened. But rejecting the broken parts locked deep inside is contrary to the way the Lord looks at those same places. He loves every part of you and wants to redeem your entire life, not to reject or judge it.

Acceptance

We must, with the Holy Spirit's help, approach our broken past the way Jesus engaged with broken people. Consider Zacchaeus, the woman caught in adultery, the Samaritan woman, and the Gadarene demoniac. Each of these individuals was

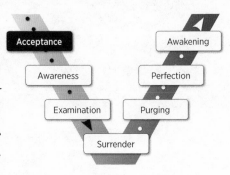

broken and had made sinful choices. Yet the Lord approached them with acceptance and love. He did not come to condemn people, but rather to set them free to be God's dear children (John 3:16–17).

While the Lord's attitude enraged the religious leaders of his day, Jesus was unrelenting in his love and care for the lost and broken. Jesus made it clear that he did not come to the world to serve as judge, but rather as a physician to those in need (Luke 5:31). Though he had every right to reject sinners, he never did. He came preaching, "Repent," but he moved toward sinners with love and acceptance. If we want to walk as Christ did, then his attitude toward brokenness must be our own.

We must be careful at this point. By taking a stance of judgment and rejection toward our own brokenness and weakness, we can be cutting off a part of ourselves essential to our wholeness. Sometimes we go beyond wanting our sinful past eliminated to wanting to cut out the parts of ourselves that made those choices.

Jesus does not share that desire. He wants these parts redeemed and secured in our identity as God's dearly loved children.

Jesus desires to wrap every part of who we are in the arms of God's grace. A time comes when we must extend that same grace to ourselves. That Christlike stance will welcome the broken parts of ourselves out of hiding and into the light of transformation where Jesus can cleanse and heal us from the garbage and debris that choke out who we truly are.

The first stage in our journey of descent (as depicted on the V diagram on page 51) is Acceptance. Choosing the stance of acceptance and love is not easy. It demands courage and faith. Yet when we do take that risk, we begin a journey that will secure our lives and awaken the wonder of who God created us to be.

Awareness

This is the second stage of descent toward healing. Jesus asked, "Can the blind man lead the blind? Will they not both fall into a pit? ... Why do you look at the speck of sawdust in your brother's eye and pay no attention to the plank in your own eye? How can you

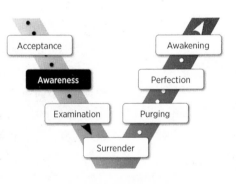

say to your brother, 'Brother, let me take the speck out of your eye' when you yourself fail to see the plank in your own eye?" (Luke 6:39, 41–42).

There are several lessons in these words from Christ, but the central truth is about self-awareness. Jesus describes a vaudevillian-like sketch in order to demonstrate how absurd it would be to watch a person attempting delicate eye surgery while maneuvering around a giant plank in his own eye. Jesus is not simply highlighting how ridiculous this would be, but also how impossible. Through well-constructed hyperbole, Jesus is pointing out how absurd it was that a person did not recognize the problem sticking right out in front of him.

It would seem that this level of blindness would be impossible. But many of us have embraced beliefs about ourselves and dysfunctional behaviors that are just as destructive, yet we do not recognize them as problematic. We have responded to and controlled our world in these ways for so long that we do not see how they are keeping us from the freedom that is ours as children of God. Many of our responses and reactions are unhealthy and hurtful, both to ourselves and others, but such behavior has become so natural and automatic that we have lost awareness of it.

The following quote from R. D. Laing is instructive on this point. He wrote: "The range of what we think and do is limited by what we fail to notice. And because we fail to notice what we fail to notice, there is little we can do to change; until we notice how failing to notice shapes our thoughts and deeds."[1] Awareness as described in this step on the journey of descent means opening our eyes with an attitude of love and acceptance to the dysfunctional ways in which we seek to control and manipulate our world. We must recognize that these actions are driven by identity insecurity that results from believing we simply do not measure up.

The message that we do not measure up causes us to construct a rather sophisticated approach to managing life. We do this in an attempt to get what we so desperately need. In my own brokenness, I learned to dominate when necessary, control and manipulate, intimidate if needed, and perform to meet core longings. When triggered, I lashed out in anger, withdrew into myself, became self-abusive at times, and hid. For years, I did this rather automatically, spontaneously. The time came, however, for my own journey of descent, and self-awareness was a painful-yet-necessary early step on that journey.

Self-awareness means increasing in self-knowledge, discovering how you respond and relate to the world around you. It is an attitude of openness and acceptance toward yourself, grounded in grace and love. The knowledge gained through self-awareness clears a path before you for genuine growth and freedom. Thomas à Kempis, a fifteenth-century follower of Christ, once wrote, "True self-knowledge is the highest and most profitable discovery in all of life."[2]

You must ask the Holy Spirit to help you see the dysfunctional behaviors you use to get what you need or to kill the pain of not getting what you want. Awareness is the ability to step back and take notice. In this case, you are taking notice of reactions, strategies of control, behaviors of domination, discounting actions, aggression, sinful dependencies, and much more. You need to recognize these strategies of brokenness and come to realize that they have cost you dearly. The Spirit will lead you down this path and support you as you cry out, "Help me, Lord."

Examination

Awareness focuses on the un-healthy responses and reactions we embrace to control our world, especially those growing out of the identity message that we are not enough. At the stage of

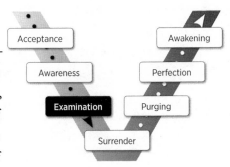

awareness, we are asking the Lord to open our eyes to see the "what" of what we do. As the V diagram illustrates, examination takes us deeper on the journey of descent. It is, with the help of the Holy Spirit, a careful, discerning look at what drives these choices and behaviors in the first place. It is, if you will, a hard look at the garbage and debris that hinder our ability to stand secure on our identity as children of God.

Examination focuses on the why.

- Why do I do these things?
- What drives the reactions that rise up so quickly, so powerfully?
- What is it that empowers the dysfunctional behaviors I so consistently engage in?
- Where are the brokenness, weakness, and sinfulness that dwell beneath the way I am living my life?

This is not an easy step. At the same time you welcome this journey, there will be resistance. This is understandable. You especially need the Presence and strength of the Holy Spirit. It is equally essential that you maintain the Christlike attitude of love and acceptance toward yourself. You are God's child, dearly loved and desired. You dare not take any other stance toward yourself than the one our Lord takes. A grace-saturated embrace is the foundation of this part of the journey.

During the stage of examination, the focus will be primarily on three main issues. I have written extensively about each in three other books, *Wounded, Draw Close to the Fire,* and *Healing Care, Healing Prayer.* These resources not only provide more extensive definition of these matters, but they also provide guidance regarding a pathway of healing in the Presence of Christ. Here, I will provide a basic explanation of the source of brokenness, weakness, and sinfulness that drives the dysfunctional choices people make in life.

Ungrieved Loss

The first category of brokenness (defined earlier as debris) that keeps us from living out of our identity as God's own children is ungrieved loss. I am convinced, after working with hundreds, if not thousands, of people seeking healing, that every loss in life demands an appropriate season of grieving. I will go even further to say that this principle stands true whether you have lost your favorite person or your favorite pen. Ungrieved loss has a devastating impact on people emotionally, psychologically, relationally, physically, and spiritually.

A tragic story is recorded in 2 Samuel 13. David's son Amnon creates a ruse in order to get close to his half-sister Tamar. She comes to his bedroom to help him when he feigns sickness, but he rapes her. Amnon then casts her aside brutally, leaving Tamar deeply wounded and completely devastated. She tells her brother Absalom what happened, and he gives her the worst possible advice. He instructs her to keep quiet. The last we hear of Tamar in the Scriptures is that she went to live with Absalom, "a desolate woman."

Failure to grieve may birth devastating consequences. It results in despair, anger, even depression. It can lead to acting out, lashing out, and hiding out. Losses put away without grieving grow like black mold in darkness. Soon a person will have trouble breathing freely. Ungrieved loss never bears good fruit.

God welcomes our grief. He wants us to pour out our hurts and losses before him, no matter how insignificant we might believe them to be. Over one third of the psalms are songs of disappointment and grief. Read Psalm 109. You will see that the Lord welcomes you to cry out before him honestly, uncensored, and with all the emotion pent up inside. Ungrieved losses build up inside us like debris. The Lord wants to meet us there, receive our heartbreak, and free us to live our lives in our true identity as children of God.

False Beliefs

Remember Cathy Tustin from the previous chapter? Her life was compromised by the presence of false beliefs. Cathy was told, in multiple ways, that boys are more important than girls. Through words and deeds her parents communicated that boys are worth big investments from parents. She, however, was simply not enough. This false belief led to great pain and dysfunction in Cathy's life. No matter how hard she worked to try and prove her parents wrong, deep inside she believed what they said about her, and she lived in the resulting insecurity.

False beliefs, the second category of brokenness that must be examined, are a huge issue with countless Christians. Many false beliefs are instilled as a result of words, sometimes by the failure to speak certain words, and more often than not they are the ugly fruit of wounding experiences in life. I have listened as people described devastating lies that drove destructive behaviors in good people. Phrases such as, "You are stupid," "You have horses--t for brains," "You will never amount to anything." Countless discounting and demeaning messages have been spoken to people and implanted in them, often when they are young and vulnerable.

Other false beliefs take root, not because of words, but events. How many adults have carried the devastating false belief that their parents' divorce was their fault? I have spoken with more than a few women who were abandoned by a father, only to conclude that they were unlovable, were not worth staying for, or that all men leave and even God can't be trusted. These false beliefs are destructive and drive a great deal of emotional upheaval and dysfunctional behavior in Christians' lives.

Like ungrieved loss, false beliefs accumulate deep within and must be recognized. Through the power of the Holy Spirit and through the transforming work of Christ, we must be released from these false beliefs. Through the same spiritual encounter we must hear the Lord speak into our souls the truth of our value, acceptance, worth, and wonder. This cleansing replacement makes it possible to awaken to the beauty of who we are as cherished sons and daughters of God.

Wounds

A third and final category of brokenness to be examined on the journey of descent is wounding. People walk around daily with debilitating hurts from emotional wounds, great and small. Some of these wounds were self-inflicted and, unprocessed with the Lord, they continue to bring great pain. Countless wounds occurred, whether intentionally or unintentionally, at the hands of others. Often, they happen as a result of experiences with people who were supposed to nurture, care, and protect, and did not.

In my book *Strong Winds & Crashing Waves,* I developed a nonclinical description of wounding, identifying categories to help people better understand. There are Wounds of Withholding, when caregivers fail to provide what is essential to physical and emotional development. Protection, nurture, encouragement, affirmation, and delight are examples of such care, and when withheld, their absence deeply compromises emotional development.

Wounds of Aggression, on the other hand, represent more than failing to give what a child needs. Caregivers give what is not needed, such as any level of abuse. Criticism, discounting, or emotional and physical abandonment wound people and compromise well-being. Even with the passing of years, unaddressed wounds like these impact the way people view God, view others, and most critically, view themselves.

A third category of wounding would be Wounds of Betrayal. This represents wounds that occurred when people with stated power and authority abused their position. It happens when a teacher abuses a student, a nurse abuses a patient, a pastor a parishioner, or a police office a citizen. Power given to care and protect was used instead for personal gain or control. This wounds deeply, especially so because of the unequal distribution of power.

Event Trauma, a fourth category of wounding, occurs when circumstances outside the normal range of human experience suddenly crash in. Illness, natural disaster, automobile accidents, and the like break through the veil of control and can bring not only physical, but emotional harm to people. Such events often traumatize and, when unprocessed, leave great levels of insecurity and fear in the wake.

Such wounds contribute to the accumulating heartache that exists deep within so many Christians' lives. Even when people work hard to put all this behind them and try to look toward tomorrow, these may cast a shadow. Wounds must be processed and transformed by Christ. When that happens, the foundation of identity is accessible for people in new, exciting, and freeing ways.

Surrender

At the deepest level of our journey of descent is the stage labe-
led Surrender. The concept of
surrender does not seem like an
admirable quality. It conjures up
notions of giving up, throwing
in the towel, and defeat. I understand that. We can identify more

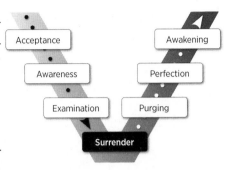

than a few situations in life where surrender is the very last thing a
person should do. The words of Winston Churchill come to mind.
He provided the moral courage for an entire nation, telling the
British people who were being pounded daily with German bombs,
"We shall defend our island, whatever the cost may be, we shall
fight on the beaches, we shall fight on the landing grounds, we
shall fight in the fields and in the streets, we shall fight in the hills,
we shall never surrender."[3]

Surrender to the will of God, however, is another matter.
George Matheson was a nineteenth-century Scottish pastor, author,
and hymn writer. Amazingly, even though he went blind when he
was twenty years old, he did not surrender to his circumstances
but became a widely respected religious leader in his day. He had
a profound understanding of the importance of surrender in the
Christian life. The words of one of his most famous hymns demonstrate that surrender is the posture that makes room for the Lord
to do a deep work of transformation.

Make me a captive, Lord
And then I will be free.
Force me to render up my sword,

And I shall conqueror be.
I sink in life's alarms
When by myself I stand;
Imprison me within thine arms,
and strong shall be thy hand.

These words capture the paradox of spiritual transformation. There is always a call to surrender. This surrender is not characterized by resignation, that angry "go ahead, you will do what you want anyway" attitude. It is the open hand of relinquishment, an act of extending complete submission to the Lord for him to accomplish his purpose, regardless of the cost.

Surrender is not simply a part of the journey of descent. It is the turning point. Once we become aware of how we react and seek to control our world, and recognize through examination the ungrieved losses, false beliefs, and wounds that are compromising our well-being, surrender is the first step of ascent. Surrender is by no means easy. It is an act of giving up control, all the while dealing with the broken debris that has brought unbearable pain and dysfunction to our lives. Surrender is an active choice to turn away from the values and messages of this world that have driven our performance and striving and to fall into the grace of the Father who loves us.

When I was a young boy, my mother would occasionally take my sister and me to church. The pastor preached, "You must be born again," almost every Sunday. At the end of the service he would extend an altar call, inviting people to move to the praying rail and surrender their lives to Christ. As people responded, the congregation sang the hymn, "I Surrender All," written by Judson Van DeVentor.

All to Jesus I surrender,
All to Him I freely give;
I will ever love and trust Him,
In His presence daily live.

I surrender all,
I surrender all,
All to Thee, my blessed Savior,
I surrender all.

I watched as people went forward while those powerful words were sung. Even as a young boy I had a deep sense that the people kneeling up front had reached a turning point. That turning point is precisely where we now are on the journey, asking the Lord to set us free from what was, so that we can now, in his power, take the first steps toward a new life as his secure and eternal child. Pressing beyond the desolation within, we invite the Lord to bring his healing, cleansing light into the deepest part of our soul.

Purging

Cheryl and I live on a beautiful small farm in Ohio. It has incredible trees, fields for grain farming, and a wonderful view on top of a rolling hill that drops into a gorgeous meadow. There is also an amazing barn built in 1851. Friends and family often come by to relax at our own private retreat. The farm has been the site for wedding pictures, engagements, family picnics, and more than a few campouts by students. We love our farm.

When Cheryl and I first purchased the small farm we call home, it was a mess. No one had lived there for more than two years, the land had grown up wild with briars. Every building on the property was filled with junk and in serious disrepair. Worst of all, the previous owner loved dogs. She loved them so much that she had thirty-two dogs living with her inside the house. When she left the property, she left behind a great deal of garbage, including inside the house. Truthfully, a great deal of what had been left behind was from the dogs!

Friends thought we had lost our minds. When we purchased the farm, we were in our mid-fifties and living in a beautiful four-bedroom home in a coveted part of town. The farm was a wreck, and more than a few people advised us to run. The farmhouse alone was a disaster, and you could smell it from the driveway! Yet Cheryl and I didn't simply see the farm as it was; we saw what it could become. However, before even thinking of living there, we had to work, and I do mean *work*, at cleaning up the property. Garbage had to go before the beauty of this property would ever be unveiled to our friends and family. Our lives are like that. So much trash has to be cleaned up before life can become what it ought to be.

So far, on our journey of descent, we have been touched by the matchless love of God that accepts us as we are. No judgment or rejection. We have also chosen to extend the same grace to ourselves. We then moved deeper, becoming aware of the different and dysfunctional ways in which we seek to control and react to our world. From there, we descended to ask the Holy Spirit to show us why we do these things. We wanted to see what loss, false beliefs, and lies have driven the choices we make. Finally, we reached the turning point of surrender, where we asked the Lord to have his way, his will in our lives.

Now, as we make the first move on the right leg of the V diagram to begin our ascent, we enter the stage of purging. I could have chosen another word for this step, such as *healing, cleansing,* or *freedom.* They certainly sound better and a bit more encouraging.

But for me, *purging* works best. It reflects a traditional pathway of spiritual formation that the Christian mystics called purgation. It is a time when, through relinquishment, we allow the Lord to eliminate from our lives whatever is keeping us from the

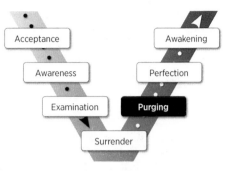

security and wonder of living out of our true identity: child of God.

As always, this is a time when we are deeply connected to the transforming work of the Holy Spirit, saying yes to a deep and not always easy season of change. Phrases that come out of Psalm 51 come to mind, informing this part of the journey.

- Have mercy, verse 1
- Blot out, verse 1
- Wash away, verse 2
- Cleanse me, verse 2
- Create in me a pure heart, verse 10
- Renew, verse 10
- Restore, verse 12

These words represent deep transformation, transformation that only the Lord can accomplish. It is possible because of surrender. Because you say yes.

The Scriptures often remind us that transformation does not come easily. The Bible speaks of such major life change using the metaphors of death, of being buried, and also of the cross. Frank Tuoti spent part of his life as a Trappist monk. From that experience he wrote a helpful book, *Why Not Be a Mystic?*, in which he reminds us, "There is nothing dramatic, or romantic about a crucifixion, especially when it is our own."[4] He went on to quote St. John of the Cross, who said: "No matter how much an individual does through his own efforts, he cannot actively purify himself enough to be disposed to the least degree for the divine union of the perfection of love. God must take over and purge."[5]

Remember, this process begins in God's grace-saturated embrace. Through the Holy Spirit you become aware of the behaviors that do not reflect your identity as God's child, and you can say yes to the cleansing of the garbage of loss, lies, and wounds that have kept you from awakening to the true self God made you to be. This step—purging—is movement toward the light, the beginning of ascent to new life and intimacy with the Lord. It is also the part of the journey where community and guidance from mature Christians best serve you.

Perfection

As we progress further on the upward leg of our V diagram, we reach the stage called Perfection. Even mentioning the word *perfection* as part of the Christian life can be frightening. I know it certainly scares me. It conjures up ideas that I need to be sinless,

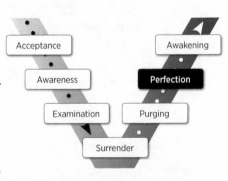

to never make a mistake, and to walk in holiness without stumble or misstep. That is definitely not what I am talking about. Any notion that you will come to the place of perfection in this life is grossly mistaken. This journey is ongoing as you visit and revisit the various stages necessary along the way. Possibly, the best way to understand this process is with the phrase, "I am transformed, I am being transformed, I am yet to be transformed!"

I use the word *perfection* because, like *purging*, it has historic roots in Christian formation. It represents the ongoing process that many call sanctification. That word, however, is loaded and can create more than a little theological debate as to what it actually entails. As such, I want to be clear from the beginning regarding my use of the word *sanctification* and the corresponding definition of *perfection*. Sanctification is best described as the process by which the Holy Spirit frees you to live as who you really are, a child of God.

This is a process, and as such it takes patience, ongoing surrender, and time. It also, as you can see in the definition, is dependent upon the work of the Holy Spirit. I encourage you to look at my book *Untamed Christian, Unleashed Church* for a fuller discussion of the Holy Spirit and his ministry in our lives. This part of the journey, sanctification, is about freeing you to live as a child of God.

More than a few Christians view this as a process of the Holy Spirit turning Christians into something they now are not: holy. I could not disagree more. Because you are in Christ, you already are holy, you share the nature of Christ, and you have been transformed into a child of God. However, the garbage of your life keeps you from living that way. Perfection is the process of the Holy Spirit freeing you, maturing you, to live out of who you already are, by the grace of Christ.

So then, what is sin? Based on what I have said previously, sin is character and conduct that does not flow out of who you truly are in Christ. Sin is driven by the garbage buried deep within your soul. Jesus, who is both the center and destination of the journey, has seen to it that you are secure, with eternal life welling up within, all flowing from your identity as child of God.

According to Romans 8:28–29, the Lord uses all things to help us live as who we truly are in Christ. God is present in all we face in life, and he chooses to use those events to perfect us in Christ—if we surrender, which again is far from easy. The Lord also frees us, matures us, as his children through the activities we embrace that are sources of his light and love. Gathering regularly with other believers in worship positions us for transformation. So does frequent prayer, as do the use of spiritual disciplines, practicing spiritual exercises, engaging in the sacraments, and faithfully meeting the Lord in Scripture.

I must be clear at this point. I do not believe that doing all these things perfects us. If they did, then our transformation would be in our hands. These activities position us to be changed by God. We position. He brings the change. We are faithful in devotional commitments because he has historically manifested his Presence in these disciplines and exercises. We should hang out where he is known to show up. When he does, we change.

The Holy Spirit uses what you offer as a pathway to freedom as God's child. Many Christians try hard to break free by their own efforts, but the presence of garbage deep within causes them to hit a wall in their spiritual lives. When you allow the Spirit to bring deep purging of the debris deep inside, he then moves through everything you offer as a pathway to transformation and perfection. You can meet God in the devotions and disciplines of the Christian life and begin to say no to the values and discounting messages of this world. You have then embraced your "somebody-ness" as God's very own.

Awakening

The first church I pastored was small, filled with some of the most wonderful people in the world. The congregation numbered fewer than one hundred, and attendance averaged about seventy-five or eighty, unless it was Christmas or Easter. Folks there were hard-working, mostly related by family, and patient with a green pastor who had only one year of seminary under his belt.

I have wonderful memories of the people from Amity. One man, Willard Hall, always brings a smile to my heart when I think of him. Willard was pleasant, faithful at our work days, generous with his time, and always had a good word. Willard was especially complimentary as he left church each Sunday, smiling and whole-heartedly saying, "Great sermon today, Pastor. Great sermon."

I appreciated Willard's enthusiasm about my preaching. However, there was one caveat to his affirmation. He slept through every sermon I preached. Week by week, as soon as I began to speak, Willard began to nod off. First his eyes would close, followed by the nodding head, slumping in his seat, and on one occasion, practically falling into the aisle. Yet, as people filed out Sunday after Sunday, Willard would smile, shake my hand warmly, and compliment my message. I appreciated the praise, but his actions left his wonderful words just a bit hollow. I would have preferred that he stay awake once in a while.

Awakening, the next movement of the journey, is the final stage of living as a secure child of God. It represents an ongoing enlightenment to the movement of God in our lives and in the world. It is not a moment in time,

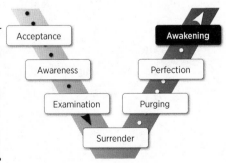

but an ongoing awakening at the deepest place of our identity, where and when the true self emerges to embrace the wonder and uniqueness present within and through the grace and love of God.

This awakening is a continuous work of the Holy Spirit, impacting not only your character and conduct, but also the depth of intimacy you experience with your Father. It represents being alive to him and with him in dimensions that are unfolding and ongoing. As you experience increased freedom from the debris that has smothered the "life" out of you, you experience awakenings that open new vistas and possibilities before you. You are by grace able to ascend into the consolation of being a "child of God."

I would emphasize that this is not about a single awakening, but instead many awakenings over time. Some aspects of spiritual awakening are connected to spiritual experiences that are episodic and memorable. Most awakenings take place moment by moment through the patient faithfulness of step-by-step awareness. Let me suggest five awakenings that unfold in this season, all empowered by the Presence of the Holy Spirit.

First, you will experience awakenings to the Kingdom of God. Jesus told Nicodemus in John 3 that seeing and entering the Kingdom demanded being born again. I believe he was speaking of spiritual awakening in our lives. Awakening to the Kingdom allows us to see the movement of the reign and rule of God. It involves entering the movement of God's Spirit on Earth, living by his values, participating in the signs and wonders of his Kingdom that are redeeming this world. This awakening, which is ongoing and unfolding, demands childlike wonder and trust in God and in his love shown in Christ.

Second, we also begin to awaken to the fullness of Christ. Paul was undoubtedly Christ crazy and believed that Jesus, and

Jesus alone, provides identity security and meaning for those who believe. That is why he wrote these words to the Corinthian church: "No matter how many promises God has made, they are 'Yes' in Christ" (2 Cor. 1:20). Here, we begin a deeper and deeper awakening to all that Christ has done for us. As Paul said in Ephesians 1:3, God has "blessed us in the heavenly realms with every spiritual blessing in Christ." How are we forgiven? Because of Christ. How do we get to heaven? By Christ. Why are we now God's children? Christ again. On and on it goes, and the more we awaken to what Jesus has done, the more secure we are in our identity.

Third, the Holy Spirit awakens us to God's Presence in every moment of our lives. We discover that he is not a distant God, inactive in our lives. We awaken to the wonder of every moment alive with him. We need not wait for someday spiritually, because we have been awakened to the now of God's Presence.

Added to this, we awaken to the Presence of Christ in the community of believers. The promise of two or three gathered (Matt. 18:20) becomes our reality. All the potential of being the "People of the Presence" begins to become our ongoing experience as his people. Church then is not a building or a service we endure, but the gathering of the faithful in the Presence of Jesus.

Ultimately, we experience the unfolding awakening of the true self. The Holy Spirit enables us to see that we are God's workmanship, fearfully, wonderfully crafted in his image. Instead of putting away our uniqueness because of a discounting and abusing world, we awaken to his handiwork in our lives, redeemed by the grace of Christ. We awaken to the breathtaking reality that Jesus lives within us, and we live within him. The light of that reality shines forth, demolishing the message of the world that says you are not enough.

This is all grace, extravagant, undeserved, and amazing. The journey has taken us to a place of freedom we did not know was possible. And by his mercy, we will go there again, and again, and again . . . and be free.

For Your Reflection

1   Why is it important that you take a stance of acceptance to begin this journey?

2   Describe your understanding of "awareness."

3   What makes examination so difficult?

4   What loss, false beliefs, and wounds has the Lord been showing you?

5   Why is it important that you walk this journey with others?

6   What makes surrender difficult?

7 What is the relationship between purging and perfecting?

8 Where do you sense awakening happening in your life?

9 What is Jesus asking of you?

Notes

[1] This quote is attributed to twentieth-century Scottish psychiatrist R. D. Laing.

[2] Thomas à Kempis, *The Imitation of Christ,* annotation by Paul Wesley Chilcote (Woodstock, VT: Skylight Paths, 2012), 5.

[3] Winston S. Churchill, *Never Give In!: The Best of Winston Churchill's Speeches, Selected by His Grandson* (New York: Hyperion, 2003), 210–217.

[4] Frank Tuoti, *Why Not Be a Mystic?: An Irresistible Invitation to Experience the Presence of God—Here and Now* (New York: Crossroad, 1996), 101.

[5] Ibid., 102.

Chapter Five

Amazing Grace

I was afraid of God as a young boy—for good reason. My mother often used the fear of God as a behavior modifier, and she painted a frightening picture of his sudden wrath. It is only fair to say that my mother had deep wounds from a painful childhood. Her mother died before my mother was two, and her dad passed away by the time she was eight. My mother was raised in the home of an aunt who already had three children of her own. Elements of abuse were not uncommon, and that, with the death of her parents, left my mother emotionally scarred.

I am not sure why, but one of the effects of her wounding was a view of God that was harsh, demanding, and punitive. This was reflected in her own parenting at times, no less than when she would bring God into the equation. I was taught that God was quick to punish for bad behavior. One of my mother's notorious warnings was that "God can knock that face off you any time he wants." Often uttered as a maternal warning for me to not get in trouble, I usually heard those words right when I was walking out the door.

I wondered why God was in to knocking faces off. Why that? What offense exactly initiates getting your face knocked off? I didn't know, and for sure I wasn't about to ask my mother. More than once, though, I would be walking down the sidewalk imagining my face suddenly rolling off in front of me. It was a frightening thought, and drawing close to God was not very inviting. I am sure it impacted my eventual experience of faith and took some time to deconstruct in my thinking.

Let's return to the oft-repeated premise that "to know God you must know yourself, and to know yourself you must know God." Depending on your view of God, that statement can either be a stepping stone or a stumbling block to being secure in your identity as a child of God. Your view of God matters, especially your understanding of his nature, his attitude toward you, and his approach to having a relationship with you.

It is not difficult to build the case that many people, including Christians, have a skewed view of God. People see God as angry, withholding, and demanding. They believe God is quick to judge and punish, requires model behavior as a precondition of blessing, and hates sin and sinner alike. The gospel many hear begins with sin and judgment, only then highlighting salvation through Christ, which, after belief, requires personal sin management. If this view is true, who would want to know God more in order to know more about themselves?

A person's view of God matters. It determines whether there is a desire to draw near or run away. More than a few times when working with people who have been emotionally wounded, I have encouraged them to ask the Holy Spirit to give them a picture of God coming close. Too many times I have had people reply, with more than a little fear, "I don't want him close. He frightens me."

Granted, God is awesome in the truest understanding of that word. His perfection and light are unapproachable and his power indescribable. It is, if you will, beyond nuclear. However, he desires intimacy with his children and demonstrates that through the Incarnation. Jesus, the Son of God, came into our world to show us the true character of our Father and draw us into his embrace.

The Scriptures are especially clear on one point. If you want to know what God is like, look at Jesus. The author of Hebrews said that "the Son is the radiance of God's glory and the exact representation of his being" (1:3). When the disciple Philip asked Jesus to show him the Father, Christ said, "Anyone who has seen me has seen the Father" (John 14:9). The incarnation of Christ was the Father's way to show his children his true nature and character. Do you want to know what God is like? Read the Gospels carefully, paying attention to everything Jesus says and does. Do this, and you will be captured by the Father's love.

Jesus was tender toward the broken and weak, and he did not reject or scold those who failed or fell along the way. He healed the sick, set people free from evil spirits, and stood between the sinful and their oppressors. Jesus never used his power for selfish gain, instead helping those who had lost their way. Jesus invited outcasts into his inner circle, ate with those others rejected and judged, and counted simple people as his closest friends. He even called his betrayer his friend. The Lord extended love generously where others dispensed hate, taught his followers to be kind and generous, and welcomed little ones into his arms.

Jesus endured ridicule because of his association with the poor and declared that the Kingdom of God belonged to people like them. He taught his followers to love and never retaliate, and even to bless those who spoke ill of them. He humbled himself to wash feet to demonstrate love in action, dispensed grace and mercy scandalously, and would not tolerate the abuse of power.

When Jesus could have called down fire from Heaven to deliver himself from the cross, he stayed as an act of love. Even then he thought of others, asking the Father to forgive those who nailed him there, all the while promising a thief that he would walk with him in Paradise on that very day. At the end, he did not complain or sermonize, or speak in angry tones. Instead, he tenderly spoke of care for his mother, making sure that she would be provided for and safe. He came to earth from the heart of Love, to demonstrate Love, so that all God's children would awaken to Love and be free. He came to show us the face of God.

The Grace of Union

Yes, Jesus came to show us the character of God, and in him we see that God is love. But what was the ultimate purpose of the Incarnation? Certainly it was more than a cosmic show-and-tell. There are unsearchable riches in Christ, and each treasure flows from God's matchless grace. We know that those riches include forgiveness of sin, the indwelling Presence of the Holy Spirit, spiritual gifts, empowerment for service, and the hope of Heaven. As great as these gifts are, none represents the ultimate purpose of Christ's journey to earth.

The ultimate mission of Christ was not payment for sin, or enabling us to reach a higher moral standard, or the ability to spend our lives in service to his Kingdom. Each of these treasures is priceless, but I assure you they are not the end for which Jesus gave his life. Above all the riches that Christ has brought to our lives, nothing surpasses the grace of securing our identity as children of God. He came that we might experience eternal union with our Father and live in the security and wonder of that reality. "Spirit is leading us to union—to transforming, personal, intimate relationship with the triune God."[1]

Jesus told his disciples that he and the Father are one (John 10:30). Later, he prayed that his followers would experience the same love relationship he has with the Father (John 17:11, 20–23). The writer of 1 John emphasized this theme when he wrote, "If anyone acknowledges that Jesus is the Son of God, God lives in them and they in God" (4:15). Paul picks up this theme in his own writing when he declares, "I no longer live, but Christ lives in me" (Gal. 2:20). He is stating that union with Christ is the goal of Christian living, which then brings us into union with the Father. That is the gift of being declared a child of God.

Brennan Manning, author, former Franciscan priest, and self-declared ragamuffin, said that "union not only transcends every political, social, cultural, and religious consideration and not only infuses them with ultimate meaning, but defines the very purpose of life itself."[2] Manning believed that the invitation to union was not reserved for those Christians who are diligent to follow all the rules, observe all the rites, and fulfill all the religious obligations laid out before them. Instead, he insisted that "the Love of Christ embraces all without exception."[3]

Relationship

There are three dimensions to the union Christ has provided by grace through faith. The first dimension of union is relationship.

In his important work, *The Crucifixion of Ministry*, Andrew Purves shared the stunning truth that what is true of Christ by nature as God's Son now becomes true of us through adoption.[4] Think about this, because the implications are profound. We have been adopted as God's children. That is our identity, which secures for us an eternal relationship with God. Paul stated in Galatians 4:4 that this adoption is the very reason Jesus was born of a woman. It is about relationship.

Union means that we get to enter a relationship with God that enables us to share in the divine nature. Peter wrote: "His divine power has given us everything we need for a godly life. . . . He has given us his great and precious promises, so that through them you may participate in the divine nature" (2 Pet. 1:3–4). Simply stated, we have been brought into union with God, and we are his children. We are his children on good days and bad, when we walk in holiness or make mistakes, when we act like his children and even when we do not. That is the strength of what Christ has done, and nothing will change that. As Peter said, we can in Christ get all we need, which includes having our deepest longings met in God. This is ours through faith, and that relationship does not change because of our performance. God's children are secure in Christ, and that is the scandal of grace.

Fellowship

A second dimension to union is fellowship. Again, Andrew Purves is instructive at this point. He emphasizes that union, secured through Christ, enables us to share in Christ's intimacy with the Father. We not only have a relationship with God, but we are invited into intimate fellowship with him as well. Purves writes: "Here is the center of Christian worship and prayer, whereby through our union with Christ we share in the filial life of love between the Father and the Son in the unity of the Holy Spirit."[5]

We now hold the possibility of ongoing growth in fellowship with the Father through the indwelling ministry of the Holy Spirit. John the Beloved wrote about this fellowship in his first epistle when he said, "We proclaim to you what we have seen and heard, so that you also may have fellowship with us. And our fellowship is with the Father and with his Son, Jesus Christ. We write this to make our joy complete" (1:3–4). You now have been given the opportunity to grow in ongoing fellowship with the Father through the indwelling ministry of the Holy Spirit. If and when you position yourself, you can experience increasing levels of abiding, anointing, and authority in your life as God's child.

The first dimension, relationship, is secure because of Christ and is not dependent upon our performance, goodness, or model behavior. Jesus made this so through his sacrifice. We are sons and daughters of God. Done deal. However, fellowship happens as we position ourselves to walk in Christian maturity.

Let's make this simple. Imagine that there was a son who walked away from his father in anger. Walking away, distance, even resentment and anger do not change the fact that he is his father's son. He was, he is, he always will be a son. That relationship never changes. However, he has broken fellowship. His choices have distanced him from his father, cut off the opportunity for fellowship and intimacy, and disconnected him from the blessings of that relationship.

Is not this the central point of Jesus's story we know as "The Prodigal Son"?

A son chooses to break fellowship with his wealthy father. He takes his inheritance, leaves his father's presence, and lives a broken life squandering everything his father gave him. Starving and broke, he chooses to return to the father. Now remember, he had broken fellowship and wasted his blessings. Yet, the father runs to him upon his return and the first thing the father does is to affirm his boy's sonship. He is in essence saying, "He was my son, he is my son, he will ever be my son."

His elder brother hated what his father affirmed about his wayward brother. He wanted consequences to come to bear for his brother's behavior. He believed that union, being in relationship with the father, was conditioned on good conduct. Poor performance, to him, disqualified his brother from relationship. The father was having none of that. Yes, fellowship had been broken, and that was no small matter. It was costly to the son and the father. But the relationship as his son was as secure as it had ever been.

Jesus told this story to show us the depth, breadth, and height of God's love for his children. He grieves when fellowship is broken, but in Christ he secures the relationship we have as a child of God. Many Christians do not get this and still want relationship to be conditional. However, that is not the nature of union. Union reveals the absolutely scandalous nature of God's matchless grace.

Be sure of this: the evil one does not want you or me to ever know how secure we are in Christ. He desires to get you to doubt your security and dance to the tune of religious legalism, which makes huge demands, yet delivers little in terms of the victorious Christian life. Make no mistake, the evil one does not mind religion, as long as the rituals and obligations keep people striving, performing, and living in continuous insecurity. He will work to get you to question your relationship, perform to meet core longings, and buy the lie that it is your behavior that secures you with God. That is what he tried with Jesus, and it is what he tempts you to do as well.

Stewardship

There is yet a third dimension to union. The breathtaking grace of relationship should translate into the fruit of faithful stewardship. It is the natural response to the generosity of God's overwhelming love and goodness toward his children.

A close reading of the story of the prodigal son does affirm that the wayward son was always a son regardless of his behavior. The story also identifies that stepping away from the father, while not breaking the relationship of father and son, did break fellowship. The wayward son needed to come home in order to reconnect at the level of close communion with his father.

The story of the prodigal son is equally clear about one more point. The son was a poor steward of his father's resources. He wasted vast amounts of money when he should have been faithful to expand his father's wealth. While the father was generous to place his resources at the disposal of his son, the son allowed selfishness and immaturity to squander an opportunity to display love and responsibility. Yes, he was always the son, and that would never change. But broken fellowship and poor stewardship brought less than positive consequences.

In the Gospel of Matthew, Jesus tells a story to illustrate the importance of faithful stewardship (25:14–30). A wealthy nobleman is traveling to another land, but first calls three servants to him. He gives each a portion of his wealth and instructs them to put the money to work in order to expand his wealth. When the nobleman, now king, returns, he calls for the three servants and wants an accounting of how they used his resources. Two servants doubled their master's wealth, which brought the nobleman great satisfaction and caused him to invest even more in these two servants. However the third servant hid the money the nobleman had given him and returned it to him intact but unexpanded, which greatly displeased his master.

Stewardship is part of the grace of union. The overflow of God's love should produce lives that invest in Kingdom ministry. Through union you and I are called God's own children, and all the rights and privileges of that relationship are secured through Christ. Communing with the Father in ever-increasing fellowship is our privilege as sons and daughters. We should invest deeply in the development of that intimacy. Faithful stewardship, also part of union, becomes our response of gratitude and devotion. Relationship, fellowship, stewardship. These are the elements of the grace-filled union our Lord came to provide.

Jesus and the Wilderness

One of the most instructive biblical narratives regarding union with God comes from the combined stories of the Lord's baptism and his time in the wilderness. Both stories are found in the Gospels of Matthew, Mark, and Luke, and share the basic elements of what happened. A close reading, and in this case retelling, unearths key principles of relationship, core longings, and the strategies of the evil one to get God's children to question their identity and to compromise their inheritance.

John the Baptist had been baptizing people in the Jordan River. He preached a baptism of repentance, and people were coming to him in great numbers. The religious leaders also came to the Jordan River, but not for repentance. John the Baptist called them on their hypocrisy, referring to them as a brood of vipers.

One day while John was preaching and baptizing, Jesus arrived. John had spoken of the coming Messiah to the crowd, saying that one more powerful than he would come and baptize them with fire (Luke 3:15–18). Jesus stood before John to be baptized. Jesus did not stand on the bank with the religious leaders who believed they were above the others. Jesus stepped into the water, numbering himself among the sinners.

We must not lose or overlook this point. Jesus entered the world as a human in order to walk in our steps. He experienced life not only with us, but on our behalf. He who was perfect numbered himself among the sinners in order that we, the sinful, could be called the children of God. Jesus lived a perfect life and then by grace assigned our names to that life, while taking our broken life on as his own at Calvary. Think about the magnitude of the grace. It is not only amazing, it is scandalous.

As Jesus came up out of the water, the heavens opened and a voice spoke out of the heavens. God said, "You are my Son, whom I love; with you I am well pleased," and the Holy Spirit descended upon him as a dove (Luke 3:21–22). We must not fail to understand what took place in this moment. Remember, Jesus was numbered among the sinners and had done nothing notable to this point in his life.

There were no sermons yet, no miracles, no crowds. As far as the other people there were concerned, Jesus was simply another sinner getting baptized. He was one of them. Yet, at that very point, three monumental gifts were given to him by the Father. God declared that Jesus was his Son. He said that he was pleased with Jesus. God also filled him with the Holy Spirit, symbolized by the descending of the dove from heaven.

Okay, one more time for emphasis. Before Jesus had done anything in his ministry, while being numbered among the sinners, God made it clear that he loved Jesus, was pleased with him, and chose to empower him to live out the Father's will. Loved, chosen, empowered. This story is about identity, it is about relationship, and it is about God's love and the provision of the Holy Spirit as foundational to being his children.

God is speaking through this Scripture. While you are yet numbered among the sinners, before you have done anything to earn or deserve his love, he declares, "I love you, I choose you, and I give you my Spirit." God does this because of Christ, who lived a perfect life and then assigned your name to that life. This happens supernaturally as you place your faith in Jesus. It is the gift of grace. In Christ, God loves you before you are lovable, he chooses you before you are acceptable, and he empowers you even before you are responsible. Why? Because you are his child.

This is hard to fathom. I know myself, at least in part. I am broken, I fall short of living as a child of God in Christ, and I wander away from God's embrace as much or more than I run to him. I have done nothing to earn such favor, cannot live up to his generosity, and am often more selfish than selfless. Why would a perfect God be so loving to me? Why would he love you that way as well? The answer is really rather simple. Jesus.

The foundation of the story of Jesus and his baptism is one of union. God was declaring that he and Jesus were in relationship and that through the Holy Spirit all the longings of his life would be satisfied. In the Father, Jesus would find security, acceptance, significance, and purpose. Christ's identity was Son, and the resources of the Father were now his.

What was true of Jesus is now true for you. Through Christ you experience union, and with union comes relationship, the invitation to fellowship, and the opportunity to be a good servant of the Kingdom. You are just as secure and just as capable of having your longings met by the Father. Your identity is child of God, and the Holy Spirit indwells you to empower you to live as who you truly are in Christ. This is the heart of the story of redemption, and this is why it is called good news. Oh, and one more thing. This is why the evil one works so hard to get you to question your true identity. He did it to Jesus in the wilderness, and he tries to tempt you in much the same way. That is where we go next: the Holy Spirit, Jesus, and the temptation in the wilderness.

For Your Reflection

1. When you think of God, what feelings arise?

2. How does a person's view of God impact his or her inner journey?

3. Why do so many people see God as judge?

4. What impact would this view of God have on their desire to draw near to God?

5. The writer of Hebrews said that Jesus is the radiance of God's glory. That being so, what do the life and teachings of Jesus teach you about God?

6. Looking at Jesus, fill in the following blank with as many words as you can

   • God is_____

7. What does it mean that the ultimate mission of Christ was to bring you into union with God?

8. What is your understanding of the three dimensions of union:

   • Relationship

   • Fellowship

   • Stewardship

9. What does the story "The Prodigal Son" tell you about union, fellowship, and stewardship?

10. Spend some time meditating on the story of the Lord's baptism. Think about the principles shared in this chapter. Picture yourself there, numbered among the sinners, standing in the water, and hearing God say, "I love you, I choose you, I give you my Spirit." Imagine this over and over

again, because everything about this is true of you because of Christ.

Write down the feelings that arise in you as you do this.

I encourage you to repeat this simple phrase: "I am a child of God, I am loved, I am chosen, I have God's Holy Spirit living in me."

Notes

[1] Clark Pinnock, *Flame of Love: A Theology of the Holy Spirit* (Downers Grove: InterVarsity Press, 1996), 149.

[2] Brennan Manning, *The Furious Longing of God* (Colorado Springs: David C. Cook, 2009), 59.

[3] Ibid., 60.

[4] Andrew Purves, *The Crucifixion of Ministry: Surrendering Our Ambitions to the Service of Christ* (Downers Grove: IVP Books, 2007), 71.

[5] Ibid., 71.

Chapter Six

Idols of the *Heart*

No one likes to be duped. It leaves a bad taste in your mouth and usually conjures up that lethal combination of feelings—anger and embarrassment. Even common definitions of the word "duped" make you cringe: swindled, deceived, defrauded, misled, hood-winked, and the all-time worst, suckered. It's an ugly experience regardless of the form it takes, making it hard for even the best Christians not to retaliate with at least a good old poke in the eye.

I remember how hurt my youngest daughter Emily was when she got duped. She had moved to Virginia for her first job and was working hard to make ends meet. Emily had listed an expensive gown online, hoping to sell it as a way of helping with bills. Emily quickly had a buyer who sent her a check, with the agreement that Emily would then send along the dress. Pretty straightforward.

But when she received the check, it was for twice what Emily had requested.

Emily did not have a suspicious bone in her body. She emailed the buyer, telling her that the check was for too much money. The buyer, who was very nice to her, told Emily to send her a check back for the overpayment, along with the dress. Sounded good to Em, so off the dress and check went. However, the check she had in her hands was a fraud. It was worthless and bounced all the way back home when she tried to cash it. Emily was a victim of a scam. She had been suckered!

Emily called her mother and me in tears. She had gone to the police, who were great about telling her how gullible she was, listing every mistake she made. The money was gone, the dress was sent, and her heart was broken. Our daughter was angry, embarrassed, and in some sad way aware that not everything or everyone should be trusted at face value. Her mother and I agreed to share the financial loss with her, but unfortunately she still had to bear the hard lesson of being duped.

Do you know what is even worse than being duped? Becoming the object of ridicule and laughter as a result. That stings, and stings badly. My first memory of being duped and then laughed at came at the hands of my grandfather. I was just a little kid, and for some reason he had been given the responsibility to watch me that day. I thought it was going to be great—an entire day with Grandpap Til, as we called him. It did not turn out so great.

Very early in the day Grandpap told me that if I were good all day, he would treat me to the "blanket show." I had no idea what a blanket show might be. Maybe it was some kind of drive-in movie, or possibly being allowed to sleep under the stars, or some other adventure. To a young boy, it sounded exciting. After all, this was my Grandpap promising something special, just for me.

The day was long, and as is true of boys, I got fidgety and more than once came close to getting into trouble. Each time I did, I was reminded, "You better be good. You don't want to miss the blanket show." Those words brought me right back in line, helping me spend an entire day as the picture of decorum. Well, almost. The day wore on and my hopes grew. They grew all the way into late evening, until my excitement turned to profound disappointment.

Night came and my grandfather told me it was time for bed. "But what about the blanket show?" No response. Grandpap took me up the steps to their bedroom and insisted that I climb into bed. Had I done something wrong? Did I disappoint him somehow? I wasn't sure what had happened. So, I lay in the large bed and asked him one more time. "Grandpap, what about the blanket show?" My grandfather smiled, lifted the quilt that sat at the end of the bed, and said, "Here it is, Terry, the blanket show. It's time to go to sleep."

As the light went out, so did my joy. I had been duped. Suckered, hoodwinked, misled, deceived, defrauded, all rolled into one cruel moment. Talk about the wool being pulled over a small boy's eyes. I was so disappointed. I am sure tears formed in my eyes. I was a kid who had waited all day, worked hard to be good, and thought something special was coming my way. Instead, I painfully discovered that this was a huge joke, and I was the punchline.

It did not end there. This story, repeated by my grandfather to friend and family alike, became the source of great laughter. For years afterward I would be reminded as someone with a wry smile would say, "Hey, Terry, have you been to the blanket show lately?" I learned to smile back and say, "Yeah, every night." They laughed, I remembered, and a lump formed in my throat.

A young boy, duped by his grandfather in a way that to his grandfather was funny, but to that boy broke trust. I used to hate it when anyone brought up that experience, but I have matured. I forgave his senseless trick, though he died soon after that memorable night. In a world of evil and darkness, this was really not a big deal. That is unless you were that boy. It mattered. Being duped always matters. As for me, I became a bit warier of promises. I am sure you understand why.

The Wilderness

Jesus had an amazing experience at the Jordan River on the day of his baptism. What an unparalleled moment! The sky opened, the dove descended, and the Father spoke. "You are my Son, whom I love; with you I am well pleased" (Luke 3:22). Loved. Chosen. Empowered. This was a declaration of union with God.

God announced that Jesus was his child, he was in relationship with him, and, through the empowerment of the Holy Spirit, Jesus would walk in fellowship with the Father. God's word sealed the deal that all Jesus's core longings would be met in him. His identity was Son, his security assured, his significance rock solid, and his acceptance proclaimed in heaven and on earth. That is what the Father of Love does for his child and his children.

Jesus must have been filled with joy unspeakable. The Scripture says that he left the Jordan full of the Holy Spirit (Luke 4:1). If you have ever been full of the Holy Spirit, you know what that feels like. It is indescribable. There is joy for sure, but also this incredible sense of harmony with God. He feels so close, and you are focused, desiring only what he desires, longing for little more than being one with him. It is a spiritual experience that spills over into the physical, the emotional, even the relational. This is my own weak way of explaining being full of the Spirit, and for Jesus it must have been multiplied exponentially.

This is what God wants us to experience when we rest secure in our identity as his children. There should be—will be—joy. Knowing that we are loved, chosen, and empowered by the Spirit fills us with the indescribable. Union like this brings harmony, and hope, and a perceived-yet-unexplainable nearness to the Father. Like Jesus, we can be full. Full of the Holy Spirit, full of the love of God, and full of confidence that our deepest longings can be met in him. We are his children, and our uniqueness and gifting can be built on that reality.

But there is more to the story. Jesus left the river full of the Spirit, and it was this same Spirit that led him into the wilderness. The evil one was there, and he had one thing in mind: the same thing he has in mind for you and me. He wanted to dupe Jesus, to get him to question the union God had just declared to be true. He wanted Jesus to meet basic core longings in a deal with the devil, a deal many of us make again and again.

Satan's Lures

Many preachers and teachers have emphasized that the key lesson from the story of Jesus in the wilderness is the importance of using God's word to counteract Satan's lies. This is certainly important, and we do see in the Scriptures that Jesus responds this way to each offer Satan makes. When Satan tempts Jesus at the height of his hunger to turn stones into bread, Jesus quotes Deuteronomy 8:3, "Man does not live on bread alone."

Satan takes Jesus to a high place and shows him all the kingdoms of the world. He tempts Jesus a second time, offering him authority over these kingdoms if Jesus will bow and worship him.

Again, Jesus rebukes Satan with God's word, quoting Deuteronomy 6:13: "Fear the LORD your God and serve him only." Finally, Satan takes Jesus to the top of the Temple and challenges him to test God's promise of protection for his children, a promise God made in Psalm 91:11–12. Again, Jesus turns to Scripture, quoting Deuteronomy 6:16: "Do not put the LORD your God to the test." With that, Satan has enough, and for the moment leaves Jesus.

Using God's word against Satan's temptations is a great strategy. We need to do that, just as Jesus did. Let us, however, not fail to look beneath that tactic to the object of Satan's temptations. In two instances the devil tried to get Jesus to question if he really was the Son of God (Luke 4:3, 9). This was fundamentally about identity security. God had declared that Jesus was his Son, and Satan wanted Jesus to question that, or at least to try out his power to see if it were true.

In order to get Jesus to question, or at least to test to see if his sonship was real, Satan appealed to core longings. Jesus was hungry, so Satan wanted him to turn stones into bread. Jesus came to bring the Kingdom of God to the world, so Satan offered Jesus an easy way to accomplish that by worshiping him. Satan offered Jesus a crown without a cross. Finally, Satan appealed to safety and security, tempting Jesus to test God's word and see if God would really protect him.

This is the nature of temptation, and Satan's tactics are twofold. First, the evil one seeks to blind us to who we truly are in Christ. He has infiltrated the values of this world, he is the power behind every effort to communicate that "you are not enough, you do not measure up." He does not want us to know that we are loved, chosen, and empowered. Instead he works, in countless ways, to convince us that we are undesirable, unacceptable, and incapable.

Second, Satan takes aim at our deepest core longings. This is what he did with Jesus, and he does the same with us. Nothing reveals identity security or insecurity more clearly than how we respond to temptations aimed at core desires. Every day the evil one works to get us to seek security, significance, acceptance, and purpose apart from God. He wants us to turn to other people, professions, money, titles, and countless other entities. He wants us to exhaust ourselves through performance, working hard to prove that we do measure up, that we are enough.

Here is the saddest part of all of this: nothing Satan offers works. Oh, it may for a moment feel good to earn, achieve, and accumulate. But it does not last long. Satan offers a counterfeit that in the end is empty. Buy his offer and, like our dear Emily, you are duped! Deceived, defrauded, misled, hoodwinked, and suckered. When you realize that fact, often too late, the laughter and ridicule begin as Satan shifts from tempter to accuser. Unfortunately, because these core longings are so deep, he changes tactics a bit and works to get us to jump on the treadmill one more time. And, if we do not know who we are in Christ, we climb back on.

Satan's lures are aimed at human longing.[1] That image from Alicia Chole says it all. I love her use of the word *lure*. Loving to fish, I get what she is saying. A lure has one purpose. It is designed to catch something that is free in order to possess it. What makes a good lure? It has to appeal to what it is trying to capture. It must look like it can satisfy what the fish most wants. The fish is hungry, it wants to eat, and the lure must promise to satisfy that hunger. To attract the fish, the lure must look like the real thing, move like the real thing, wiggle to capture attention, and most of all it needs to shine.

A fish must be surprised when, after thinking it is about to dominate and get a great meal, it winds up with a barbed hook in its mouth and is being taken on a journey not of its own choosing. The master suddenly becomes the servant, and only then does it realize, if fish actually do realize, that the alluring lure was a fake all along.

I have bit down hard on Satan's lures far too many times. I have believed the message of the world, that being me is not enough, so I chased after Satan's lures. I have performed, achieved, and accumulated in an effort to be somebody, to be secure. The evil one never used bad things to get me. It all looked great, and for a moment it tasted great. But what he offered never satisfied, and rather than set me free, it only enslaved me all the more.

Ezekiel 14

I was ambushed by Ezekiel 14 recently. I had read the chapter many times in the past, but this time, it got me. It talks about how the Israelites had gone astray and about God's determination to bring them back. He stated, "They will be my people, and I will be their God" (14:11). His concern was that they had "set up idols in their hearts and put wicked stumbling blocks before their faces" (14:3). Their actions were evil, and God wanted to recapture the hearts of his people (14:5).

What exactly are idols of the heart? He is not talking about little statues that we might worship, nor is he referring to false gods. An idol of the heart is anything we turn to other than God himself for security, significance, acceptance, and purpose. If we believe more money means more security, it can become an idol of the heart. Believing that degrees make a person significant can result in the same thing. If we rely on appearance, wit, relationships, or abilities to prove our worth, then our hearts are filled with idols.

In 2 Kings the Scriptures say, "Even while these people were worshiping the LORD, they were serving their idols" (17:41). In this case the idols were physical false gods, but the statement is convicting for those who follow Christ today. There are many who love the Lord, yet look to other things to secure their lives. Yes, we believe the gospel of Christ, at least in part. We read our Bibles, go to church, even serve the Lord. Yet we keep believing that we do not measure up as we are, and we work to the point of exhaustion trying to satisfy our deepest longings.

When we do that, we are allowing other things, even good things, to capture parts of our heart that rightly belong to God alone. We are his children. That is our identity. And our deepest longings are to be met in God and God alone. The presence of these idols of the heart is in part why we ask the Lord to take us on the inner journey. We do this with the help of the Holy Spirit through acceptance, awareness, examination, and surrender (the steps we looked at earlier on the V diagram).

What about the "wicked stumbling blocks" Ezekiel mentioned? What are they? A great deal of our brokenness comes when we work hard to satisfy the core longings of our lives. Our strategy for accomplishing this impossible task involves what is by now becoming a familiar list to us—things such as performance, people pleasing, prestige, possession, and power. Satan deceives us into believing that these are stepping stones to securing our identity and deepest needs.

The evil one wants to dupe us. He works to tempt (invite) us to choose against what God has already declared to be true. God says you and I are loved, chosen, and empowered, and that through his

Spirit our deepest longings can be met. Satan, on the other hand, has twisted the values of this world, which bombards us with the message that we need to measure up. He sets before us the false promise that (here's that list again) performance, people pleasing, prestige, possessions, and power will lead us to a free life.

These are not stepping stones. They are wicked stumbling blocks. Sure, they are enticing, and they promise great gain. Paul knew this. He bought the false promise that being hyperreligious was the way for him to please God and secure his identity. In Philippians he listed at length what he had done to make himself somebody in the eyes of religious leaders. But upon finding Christ, Paul called all of this garbage, trash he was glad to see eliminated from his life so that he might gain Christ Jesus as Lord (3:1–10).

Paul went on to say that everything he needed he found in Christ. His identity was secured, not by religious striving, but through faith in what Jesus did in coming to Earth to become human. For Paul, identity security and core longings were met in one place: Jesus. This is why he wrote, "I want to know Christ— yes, to know the power of his resurrection and participation in his sufferings, becoming like him in his death, and so, somehow, attaining to the resurrection from the dead" (3:10–11).

Paul looked back on all his efforts to secure his life and found the investments wasted. He had been duped. We know how that feels. Christ set Paul free from all that garbage, unleashing new freedom in him and awakening his true self. Isn't that exactly what we need? No more idols of the heart. No more deep investments in stumbling blocks. No more biting down on the evil one's lures that enslave and defeat us.

Jesus calls you to join him in believing that God and God alone secures your identity and satisfies your deepest longings. Jesus has defeated the evil one, and now he encourages you to walk in the freedom of being God's child—loved, chosen, and empowered. Jesus wants you to never doubt what God has declared to be true: You are his child. His Spirit lives within you. Your identity is rock solid and, no matter how loudly anyone shouts otherwise, you can know it is a lie. You will not be duped!

No one gets to define you but Jesus.

For Your Reflection

1. When was the last time you were duped? What did that feel like to you?

2. Why is being duped a bad thing?

3. How did Satan try to dupe Jesus in the wilderness?

4. Why did Satan work so hard to get Jesus to question his sonship?

5. What was the relationship between core longings and the wilderness temptations of the evil one?

6. What did Alicia Chole mean when she said, "Satan's lures are aimed at human longing?"

7. What is an idol of the heart?

8. Ask the Lord if there are any in your heart.

9. What is a wicked stumbling block?

10. In what ways have you invested in performance, or people pleasing, or possessions as a way to secure your life?

Note

[1] Alicia Chole, *Anonymous: Jesus' Hidden Years and Yours* (Nashville: Thomas Nelson, 2006), 57.

Chapter Seven

All *Creation* Waits

The world has little interest in your freedom. In fact, the father of lies, the evil one, works hard to keep you chained to the lie that you do not measure up, and to the corresponding deception that in yourself you are not enough. Every strategy he employs is aimed at keeping you in the dark. He does not want you to ever discover your true identity in Christ. He much prefers that you construct a dysfunctional mechanism for controlling your world in a desperate attempt to get what you need. A common name for this mechanism is the small-ego self.

Many people talk about the false self and the true self. The idea is that a person relates in the world in ways that are not really consistent with who they are. This false self, as some suggest, becomes a dysfunctional mechanism that a person uses to pretend to be something they are not. They do this to protect themselves from deep discovery by others and to try to provide for their deepest needs. Thus, as those who promote this idea suggest, it is a false self. It is not really you.

I disagree. I contend that we develop not a false self but, instead, a small-ego self as this same maladaptive mechanism. We take pieces of ourselves and then use them dysfunctionally. We do this for the same purpose: pretense, self-protection, and providing for ourselves. We construct a way of controlling our world. It is unhealthy. It is contrary to God's plan. It is driven by brokenness. Yet this small-ego self is a part of us. It is a limited, self-serving, unhealthy misuse of who we really are.

My own wounds and sense of insignificance drove me to develop a small-ego self, just like everyone else. Messages of inadequacy and insignificance caused me to take aspects of my gifts, talents, passions, and abilities, and use these to hide what I felt others would reject in me and to promote what I believed would satisfy my core longings. God gave me these gifts and abilities because I was his child, and he wanted me to develop and use them to unleash who I really was in him and to serve the Kingdom. I instead took pieces of these gifts and constructed a way to be what others wanted me to be and to selfishly promote myself.

This way of using and limiting who I was—this small-ego self— was developed over the long journey of my life. My first memory of doing this came that day at the Finleyville bridge. Yet all through my life, as circumstances demanding performance, people-pleasing, achieving, and accumulating presented themselves, the small-ego self became further developed and more sophisticated. I used pieces of myself to construct a me that would serve and protect me in a world that said I was not enough. By doing this, I became an active participant in my own diminishment. This was the evil one's strategy all along.

Parker Palmer writes: "We arrive in this world with birthright gifts—then we spend the first half of our lives abandoning them or letting others disabuse us of them."[1] I experienced this disabuse, and quite frankly, so have you. I may not have been consciously aware of what I was doing, but I was an active participant all along. I limited who I was, manipulated who I was, and used who I was to "get home safely." The fact that this worked, at least for a while, only reinforced the process of developing this highly sophisticated small-ego self. It became my way of responding to the values of this world and its opinion of me.

You will notice that Parker Palmer mentioned abandoning and being disabused of our gifts for the first half of life. He is pointing to the fact that sooner or later life itself offers us a gift in the most unappealing wrapping. The gift comes with the face of trial, even suffering. It arrives to challenge us to lay down life as we have been living it, to step into who we truly are as children of God.

We seldom recognize these times of desolation as gifts. I certainly did not think that experiencing a deep emotional breakdown and the hospitalization that followed were gifts. I fought hard to claw my way out of both. In fact, I tried to double down on how I was already living through performance and achievement to get out of that thick darkness. By doing this, by engaging the strategies of my small-ego self, I only sank deeper into the desolation.

I had no idea that this journey of descent was actually the tender, yet severe, mercy of God inviting me to deal with internal debris accumulated through wounds, and lies, and losses in my life. God was inviting me to be free, to be who I truly was as his child. It was, as the title of Richard Rohr's book on this subject suggests, a *falling upward*.[2] It was the descent that leads to ascent. It was a deconstruction of the small-ego self, a process that reconstructs and awakens the true self.

This falling upward, or, as I prefer to call it, this awakening of the true self, is not a one-time event. Many times in our lives we will face challenges to the way we are using our gifts and abilities. Because our strategy, the small-ego self, seems to be working, we seldom surrender easily. We fear that allowing this deconstruction will leave us desperate, unable to meet the deepest longings of our lives. We hold on tighter, try harder, and perform more diligently.

The Holy Spirit beckons us to let go, to relinquish our way in order to discover God's intention for our lives, the plan he shaped before the foundation of the world. Saying yes to this divine urging unleashes possibilities for the true self to thrive. Grounded upon our identity as children of God, we are able to see, over time, our uniqueness expressed through the gifts, passions, talents, and abilities given to us by our Father. Instead of using these selfishly, we are able to enter the place of rest, being who God intended, awakened in life to the potential of serving the Kingdom selflessly, with joy inexpressible.

As I pointed out, this awakening happens over time, and certainly the journey is never easy. There will be challenges; we will experience trials. But, as Parker Palmer says, we will be able to spend the second half of life recovering and reclaiming the gift we once possessed.[3] We will move past the morass created by our own narcissism to release the wonder of all it means to be a child of God.

Paul wrote in Romans, "For the creation awaits in eager expectation for the children of God to be revealed" (8:19). Personalize this. All of God's creation can't wait to see you wake up to who you truly are in Christ. What the evil one has tried to suppress, with your cooperation, God wants to awaken and show off to his entire creation. The world needs you to be free, thriving as the child of God you are.

What nurtures and develops the awakening of the true self? At one level, countless things. Or, as Paul suggests in his epistle to the Romans, "all things" (8:28). Yet, above all other avenues of awakening, one stands supreme: love. Nothing else changes our lives or sets us free to thrive as God's children the way love does. Love is not only at the core of all our longings. Love is the emotional oxygen that nurtures the awakening and development of the true self. We must become love's captive. We must surrender to love.

Love Matters

I had the most wonderful great-aunt in all the world. Her name was Elizabeth Boss Erath, but we all knew her as Aunt Biddit. Aunt Biddit was my grandmother's sister, my mother's aunt. As a result of my grandmother's early death, before my mother was eighteen months old, Aunt Biddit was more mother than aunt to my mother. She was as warm as any grandmother could ever have been to my sister and me, a bright and shining light in our world. We often speak of how much we miss her.

Every memory of Aunt Biddit is a pleasant one. I often recall how she waited at the door, watching every car that passed by, anticipating our scheduled arrival. As soon as our car turned into the driveway, she would run out to greet us, even before the doors opened. Her squeezes were legendary, and she invariably placed her hands on each side of my face and said, "I have been on pins and needles waiting for you. You're finally here."

We no sooner entered her house than cookies, milk, and candies came out in lavish abundance. If my mother complained that

I didn't need all the fuss, Aunt Biddit quickly shushed her. "He can have anything he wants and more, for as long as he's here." Then she would look at me with her life-giving smile and say, "Right?" After a quick worried glance at my mother, I then smiled back at her and said, "Right."

In Aunt Biddit's kitchen hung a mood-o-meter. Listed round it, like hours on a clock, were various words, including "moody, angry, grouchy, gentle, kind," and so forth. It had a pointed arrow attached at the center that could be moved from one word to another. Invariably my Uncle Robb would move the hand to grouchy before I arrived. Within minutes of getting in the house, I would run to the kitchen and move it to "loving." I did this routinely all of my life, whether boy or man, and it was always met with a wink and smile from Aunt Biddit.

How well I remember the day that Aunt Biddit and Uncle Robb pulled into our driveway unexpectedly. They drove up in an old yellow Cadillac that was shined as if it just came off the factory floor. It had large sweeping fins in the rear and coned taillights. I ran to the car in surprise. Aunt Biddit's face was beaming. She opened the door and out jumped a puppy. It was little more than a crossbreed mutt, yet he was the prettiest puppy I ever saw. And he was mine. The dog jumped from the car, splashed in a puddle in our stone driveway, and then climbed all over me. That's how he got his name. Puddles.

Every time I left Aunt Biddit's home, I went away carrying a lunch she made to hold me over for the trip—a trip that took less than an hour! My lunch was filled with favorite foods and treats that I began to eat before the car pulled out of her driveway. This did not end when I grew to be a man. Even when I was married and had children, she would come to the car window with a big brown bag, hand it through the window and say, "Here, Boy, don't forget your lunch."

When it came time for me to go to college, I chose Geneva College. Truthfully, it wasn't that hard a choice, given that it was the only college that accepted me. Geneva College was a mere fifteen-minute ride from Aunt Biddit's home. This turned out to be an amazing blessing. Whether I was visiting her home, or she was bringing wonderful treats to my room, I became the envy of all my buddies. In fact, some of my friends began to stop over at her home even without me. She was that special.

All of my life Aunt Biddit brought out the best in me. Her love, her welcome, her care, stilled more than a few internal storms in my life. Regardless of how inappropriate my behavior may have been around others, I could never misbehave or be disrespectful around her. It wasn't that she demanded this. She just loved me too much for me to in any way be less than my best in her presence. I wasn't aware of it as a child, and I was too preoccupied in adolescence to notice, but as a man one thing was clear to me. Her love was an anchor holding me fast in a world that did not believe I measured up. She believed in me, and her love called out to me, "Awaken."

Loved Lavishly

Being loved well is foundational to human development. Love frees us to thrive as God's children. Every time I was with Aunt Biddit, her love summoned the best of me out of hiding, whether I knew it or not. Love was working long before I even knew love was at work. Love is like that. It is not enough that we understand love. We must open our hearts to experience love, most especially as it pours forth from the heart of our Father.

I have come to believe that many Christians who speak of the good news, the gospel, get it wrong, at least in how they shape its message. As I noted earlier, far too often communication of the gospel begins by detailing the extent of our sin and the resulting punishment. Scriptures are quoted that highlight the payment due, referred to as the wages of sin, and the corresponding death that results. Only after highlighting sin and death do they move to tell the story of Christ and God's self-giving love.

I believe this approach is incorrect at more than one point. To begin with, the matter of sin and death is, for the vast majority of people, a message that is neither news, nor is it good. Broken people are being torn apart inside, living daily with the emptiness sin brings to their lives. To tell someone that you have good news and then start with the ugliness of sin can be more than a bit confusing. It highlights a negative reality most people are painfully living out every day.

The *good* and *news* part of the gospel is found in the amazing, breathtaking, scandalous love of God that would send Jesus to earth to bring us into union with our Father. That is the heart of the gospel, no pun intended. Granted, sin and brokenness are part of the story, but they are neither the starting point nor the ending of the gospel. What captures our attention and transforms our lives is clearly the matchless, never-ending, all-consuming love of God.

Jesus was uncompromising regarding the place of love in the gospel. He said, "God so loved the world that he gave his one and only Son, that whoever believes in him shall not perish but have eternal life" (John 3:16). He went on to say in the next verse that it was not condemnation that brought him to earth but, instead, the offer of healing for the entire world. John the Apostle made this love the central theme of his first epistle to the church. He wrote that God is love (1 John 4:16), and he made it clear that the extent of God's love is seen in his sending of Jesus to set us free (4:16).

John referred to himself as "the beloved of Christ" and wrote that God's lavish love is displayed when he calls us his children (3:1). I love the concept of lavish love. It brings to mind a matchless generosity that spills over in my life, more luxurious than can be contained or explained. The proportions of this extravagant love are indescribable. This saturation of affection from the Father comes, not because of our performance or achievement, but as a grace gift for those who are his own. We are his children. John wrote, "And that is what we are!" (3:1).

St. Thomas à Kempis said of love, "Nothing is sweeter than love, nothing stronger, nothing higher, nothing wider, nothing more pleasant, nothing fuller or better in heaven or earth, 'because love is from God' (1 John 4:7). Love flies, runs, and leaps for joy. It is free and unrestrained. Love knows no limits; it transcends all boundaries."[4] God's love brings our true selves to life. The Father's love flows out of his fervent longing for you and for me. His ardent love satisfies our longings when we allow it to flow into the deepest part of our lives.

Thomas à Kempis gave words to our cry for love when he wrote, "Increase this love in me, that in my innermost being I may taste the sweetness of your love. Melt my heart that I may swim in your love. . . . Let me sing the song of your love and follow you into heaven, my beloved. Let my soul soar in your praise and rejoice in your love. Let me love you more than myself, and love myself only in you."[5]

God's love enables us to love him more, and it helps us love ourselves. We love God because we have tasted the amazing, breathtaking love he has poured into our hearts through Jesus. We are then able to love ourselves. We see that our identity as his children is rooted in the lavish generosity of his love for us. We are able to love the true self that is emerging in the oxygen of God's Fatherly, noncomparing, matchless love.

God's love enables you to see the message that you do not measure up as the lie from hell that it is. Saying no to that lie, with the help of the Holy Spirit, affirms your identity as God's child, unleashing the potential of the true self. This awakening is the fruit of union with God and is nourished by the constant stream of his love shed abroad in your heart. Love draws you into his embrace as well as drawing out of you the original wonder God placed in you before the foundation of the world.

Life as the Beloved

Henri Nouwen believed that all God's children are beloved of him. Moving this truth from a concept to an experienced reality is not easy. He said that "becoming the Beloved means letting the truth of our Belovedness become enfleshed in everything we think, say, or do."[6] Nouwen went on to share that this happens day by day, one step at a time, most often as we experience what one might call the mundane moments of life.[7]

If we are awake and aware, we will see that God's love pours out to us every day. He is present to us as we read and meditate on his Word, which should be a daily part of our lives. His love can be experienced as we worship, pray, and gather with other Christians. The Father's love is part of every good gift that comes our way, from the beauty of creation to the wonder found in family and friends. A simple act of kindness, an encouraging word, an unexpected blessing—all of these are love notes from our Father. The question is never about the presence of his love. Rather the question is, are we open and aware that he is loving us?

God's love sustains us in the difficult places, in the darker days we experience when trials weigh heavily upon us. We may not always sense his love, or even in our pain seek his love. It is there all the same, holding us fast when the storm winds blow upon our lives.

In one of my darkest hours, God's love broke through in a most unexpected, yet transforming, way. I had been experiencing dark days that overshadowed every breath I took. I was exhausted, depressed, and losing hope. I had little energy to hold on and less faith that God was holding on to me. I felt alone and could not find a path out of the desolation I was experiencing.

During that dark time, I was home alone one day and, though weary, began to pray. For whatever reason, my mind went to the Lord's crucifixion. The Holy Spirit seemed to take over my imagination, and I was picturing Jesus on the cross. The detail was unusually specific. At one point, it seemed that I was seeing Christ hanging there, his complexion washed of life, his head hanging limp at his shoulder.

I don't know how long this lasted. Regardless, I was caught in this moment in time. While I stared at Christ on the cross, my emotions were locked down. I was unmoved. That is until something happened. As I looked upon the lifeless body of the Lord, detailed within my imagination, he suddenly lifted his head and looked straight at me. His eyes penetrated me to the core, and the tender smile on his face was like a key that opened my heart.

Looking at me, Jesus said just three words: "I love you." I felt those words reach into the deepest part of my being. I was undone. I began to cry. I cried more than I had cried in years. I felt his words far more than I heard them. The love that carried them to my heart broke something free. I cannot explain what happened, but it was real, and deep, and lasts until this day. Every time I thought about this, for days and weeks afterward, my tears would flow and with that the healing went deeper. Even yet, years later, this unexpected gift of love draws me not only closer to the Lord, but also closer to my true self. This happens whenever we are ambushed by love.

In Psalm 23 David wrote poetically of the love of God. The Lord was to David a good shepherd who provided for the sheep under his loving care. David's use of this metaphor helps us to see the Lord's constant attention to the deepest needs of our lives. David speaks of being led by the Lord, nurtured, and protected. He paints a word picture of the Lord bringing us to a table set lavishly and generously. I especially love the image of a cup that runs over, a sign of goodness following God's children all the days of their lives.

Such a table has been set before you by your Father. Upon it is everything you need to satisfy your longings. You are invited to sit in fellowship with the Trinity and eat as long as your heart desires. Access to this table comes by faith in Christ, a grace-saturated gift available to you in the embrace of the Father. You must learn to come to this table, rest there, and be filled. However, there is another table. It is set by the world and is high on promise, but it delivers only exhaustion and disappointment. What follows is a discussion of these two tables, and why you must run from one and run to the other. It is a tale of two tables.

For Your Reflection

1. Where did you sense the Lord speaking to you in this chapter? What was he saying?

2. What is your understanding of the "small-ego self"?

3. Why do people construct this?

4. What parts of ourselves do we tend to use?

5. Why is it difficult to let go of the small-ego self?

6. Why must you let go?

7. What is your reaction to the notion from Romans 8:19 that all creation waits with great expectation for your true self to be revealed?

8. What was meant when it was suggested that many Christians start the gospel at the wrong place?

9. What difference does that make?

10. Were you ever loved well? If so, what impact did this have on you?

11. What did Nouwen mean when he wrote that "becoming the Beloved means letting the truth of our belovedness become enfleshed in everything we think, say, or do"?

12. What does the phrase "surrender to love" mean to you?

13. Where in your life is the Lord asking you to surrender to love?

Notes

[1] Parker Palmer, *Let Your Life Speak: Listening for the Voice of Vocation* (San Francisco: Josey-Bass, 2000), 12.

[2] Richard Rohr, *Falling Upward: A Spirituality for the Two Halves of Life* (San Francisco: Jossey-Bass, 2011).

[3] Parker Palmer, *Let Your Life Speak*, 12.

[4] Thomas à Kempis, *Imitation of Christ*, 83 (see chap. 4, n. 2).

[5] Ibid., 85.

[6] Henri Nouwen, *Life of the Beloved: Spiritual Living in a Secular World* (New York: Crossroad, 1997), 39.

[7] Ibid.

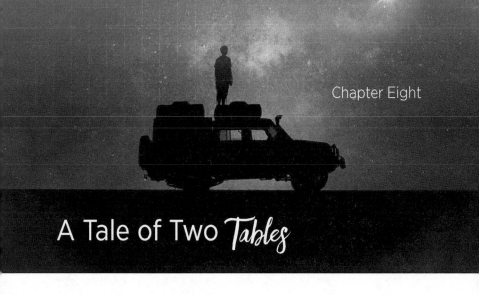

Chapter Eight

A Tale of Two *Tables*

I am a grandfather who is crazy about his grandchildren. Cheryl and I have four granddaughters and a grandson. They are unique, full of life, and give my wife and me the impression that they love to be around us. What more could grandparents ask for? The only drawback I face is that they live far away, and no matter how often we see them, it is never enough.

Ten years ago our son Aaron, daughter-in-law Destry, and two granddaughters Grace and Addison lived in the same town with us. It did not last long, but we loved those special times. The grandkids would come out to the farm, and it was only a five-minute ride to their house. We dropped in probably more than we should. Oh, well, grandparents get that privilege.

One evening Cheryl and I came to visit, and we went into the family room to love on the little ones. Cheryl was playing with

Addison, and Grace came to be with me on the couch. I was seated, so she stood next to me on the couch with her arm around my neck. Few feelings compare.

My son was the associate dean of religious life at Ashland University, and students regularly stopped by his home to hang out. We had not been there long before the parade of wonderful students began, entering through the front door, making their way to the family room. Each student that entered greeted Cheryl and me with respect, often saying, "Hi, Dr. Wardle, how are you?"

This happened several times over a period of fifteen or twenty minutes, each student referring to me as Dr. Wardle. Frankly, it was nice to be respected like that. I enjoyed the honor, especially in front of my family. I felt special. What I did notice was that Grace was taking note of how they greeted me. She would look at each student as he or she said hi, and afterward she would stare at me quizzically. One by one it happened, and the intensity of her stare fascinated me. She would look at them, then at me, with the oddest look on her face.

Then it happened. Staring at me intently, almost disapprovingly, my granddaughter weighed in loudly and clearly. She looked straight in my face, only inches away, and said, "Papa, you're no doctor. You can't fix anybody!" The room exploded with laughter, my wife and I included. At one level, Grace had not understood what the students were saying. But at another, a four-year-old hit the nail right on the head. In doing so, she leveled the playing field and exposed me for a poser! It was fun. It was memorable. It was a lesson well learned. Never place your identity in anything you can lose!

I Came to Wash Feet

The end was near, and as the Scripture records in John 13, Jesus wanted to show his disciples the full extent of his love. After the evening meal, Jesus wrapped a towel around his waist, grabbed a towel and basin, and proceeded to wash his disciples' feet. It was an amazing act of humility and affection. It was also a lesson the Lord hoped his disciples would follow.

When it came time for Jesus to wash Peter's feet, Peter protested. He just said no. Jesus was not deterred. He challenged Peter, "Unless I wash you, you have no part with me" (13:8). Peter then asked Jesus for a bath, but again the Lord was not going to be controlled or manipulated. As paraphrased with my own words, Jesus said, "Peter, I was sent here tonight to wash feet. I am not going to do less than wash feet. I am not going to do more than wash feet."

The Lord refused to compromise what he believed the Father called him to do that night. While he loved the disciples, he would not allow their agenda or their anxiety to cause him to change course. He came to wash feet, it was his offering of love, and nothing was going to get him to subtract from that mission or add to it. And it was identity integrity that held him firm in the moment.

The Scripture says, "Jesus knew that the Father had put all things under his power, and that he had come from God, and was returning to God, so he got up . . . (13:3-4). Granted, the story of Jesus washing the disciples' feet is a lesson in love and humility. No doubt. It is a model of servanthood we should and must follow. Yet a close reading of the text reveals the solid foundation that lay beneath Christ's actions. He knew who he was!

Jesus never doubted the foundation he stood upon, his identity as God's Son. This gave him the courage to resist the temptation of the evil one, and enabled him to stay true to who he was and what he was called to do. Jesus did not compromise what he knew to be the Father's will and purposes. While he loved his followers to the point of laying down his life, he did not seek to please them, perform for them, or allow their anxieties to impact his mission.

That night Jesus came to wash feet. He was not going to do less than wash feet, and regardless of Peter's anxieties and discomfort, he was not going to do more. Soon it would not be about a towel and a basin, but a lash and a cross. In both cases, Jesus, knowing who he was, where he came from, and where he was going, was able to stay true to himself and to God.

When we are not secure in our identity, it is easy to compromise in an attempt to satisfy the agendas of other people. Edwin Friedman wrote of this in his book *The Failure of Nerve*. Friedman insisted that self-definition (knowing who you are) is more important to effectiveness in leadership than expertise.[1] At one level this may seem hard to believe, especially given that many institutions of learning put a premium on competence and skill for effective leadership. Yet Friedman is right, in that an insecure leader who does not have a solid identity foundation will compromise when a core-longing need is triggered.

Friedman wrote that a person with a secure identity "is less likely to become lost in the anxious emotional processes swirling about." He described this person as "someone who can manage his or her own reactivity to the automatic reactivity of others and therefore be able to take stands at the risk of displeasing."[2] That is precisely what Jesus did. He did not cave to what the disciples did or did not want to happen that night. An insecure person might have decided to stop foot washing, or at least to find out what the disciples wanted him to do. They would have compromised. But not Jesus.

There is an interesting story in 2 Kings. Elijah had been taken to heaven in a fiery chariot, his mantle left behind for Elisha. Elijah had just crossed the Jordan River a moment before by striking his cloak on the water, and the stream had divided. After Elijah was caught up to heaven in the chariot of the Lord, Elisha grabbed the cloak, once again struck the water, and the waters of the Jordan peeled back just as before.

A band of prophets saw all this, and they tried to persuade Elisha to allow them to go looking for Elijah, believing that God might have set him down somewhere else. Elisha said no, but the prophets persisted. Finally, Elisha gave in. The Scripture says "they persisted until he was too embarrassed to refuse" (2:17). Elisha was God's child, an anointed man who would go on to do great things, much the same as you. But in this moment, he got caught up in the "emotional processes swirling about," and he compromised.

John Nordstrom is a dear friend and one of the most insightful servants of the Lord I know. His heart for Christ is huge, and his care for broken people the same. Whenever I need light for the path, John Nordstrom is one I turn to for help. John once said to me, "Conflict provokes in us either conformity or self-definition." The reactivity of others will either engage our own reactivity or cause us to stand all the more on who we are in Christ.

Truthfully, this is a mixed bag for me. Sometimes I seem able to stand and sometimes I get hooked and reactive. When that happens, I either act out or compromise. What makes the difference? For a long time I did not know. The Holy Spirit has helped me see that where I am secure as God's child and allow my core longings to be met in Christ, I stand. When a situation taps a place where I am not secure, where I still buy into the evil one's strategy, I react or compromise. It is that simple for me. It is just as simple for you.

A Tale of Two Tables

If you or I would take the time to review the choices of our lives, we would soon see that core longings motivated a great deal of what we did. I would also contend that when and where we chose based on our identity as God's children, we thrived. When insecurity motivated us, at best we survived. More often than not, choices driven by insecurity, even when we were unaware, ended poorly. We invested deeply, only to see a very poor return. Paul did this, and he called the outcome garbage (Phil. 3:8).

We must learn to stand firm on our identity in Christ and turn to God as the source of fulfilling our deepest longings. In him, as his children, we can find significance, safety, love, acceptance, and purpose. He loves lavishly and secures us eternally. We need to seek the Holy Spirit's help, learn to recognize when we are being duped, and engage deeply with our Father.

I have found the image of two tables helpful on this journey. One table is set by the world, the other by the Lord. Each offers life, yet one is based on a lie, and the other on the matchless grace of God.

The Table of the World

The world sets before us a table filled with fare that promises to bring us significance, security, love, acceptance, and purpose. We are encouraged to come to the table, but we cannot partake, at least not yet. The banners that surround this table have messages such as:

- Money can solve all your problems.
- Get a degree and find the significance you have always longed for.
- Get a nip here and a tuck there and be accepted like never before.
- Learn to win the right friends and influence the right people.
- Build bigger barns for a brighter future.
- Learn to run with the power brokers.
- Find the key to unlocking the future you always dreamed about.
- Discover the steps that take you from being a nobody to a somebody.
- Change in order to catch that special someone.

These messages, these lures of the evil one, appeal to identity insecurity. They are based on the common notion that people do not measure up, they are not enough in themselves, and therefore, their deepest core longings will never be met. That is, unless they come to the table the world sets and feast on its fare.

The question is, how does one get a seat at the world's table? The answer is quite simple. You perform, please, achieve, and accumulate. If you work hard enough, you earn a seat and partake. You make some money for security, earn degrees for significance, please the right people, look the right way, gather enough power, and you can sit down. For a while, that is.

At the table of the world, the standard is simple. The degree to which you measure up is the degree to which you partake. It is not a place of security where you earn a seat and then it is yours. No, you partake to the degree that you perform. That is the rule. Once you get to that table, you learn fast. Security gained through performance, whether the area is finance, education, relationships, or appearance, does not last. You gain a little, and then off you go to perform again . . . and again . . . and again.

Your seat at the world's table is earned and can be lost. There is zero security there. It is a place of transaction, plain and simple. You want what is on the table, so you give what the world wants from you. Relationships at this table are only necessary to the degree to which they help you earn a seat. They are a commodity, a means to a greater end.

Performing to get a seat at this table, which promises so much and provides so little, will cost you dearly. The emotional toll includes anxiety, anger, aggression, disappointment, depression, and ultimately desolation. When you confess any of these feelings, the answer that comes is, "Perform more and everything will be all right. Try even harder." In the end, the table of the world, which plays on your insecurity, will cost you everything and leave you nothing.

One more thing, changing the banners to Christian messages, placing a cross and a Bible on this table, and replacing the chairs with a kneeling rail does not make it the table of the Lord. It is still the world's table. Unfortunately, this happens all too often, another strategy of the evil one to keep God's children in bondage. The "deal," as I like to call it, is often presented to the insecure, promising that "if" you do this, "then" God will do that. Perform, please, achieve, and accumulate are still the standards. Rules, rituals, religious obligations. and rites become the means of exchange.

Those promoting this table in the name of Christ use Christian language and metaphors, and they put big money on the game. They talk about getting to heaven, forgiveness of sin, spiritual maturity, even healing and deliverance. The pathway, however, is performance, and the demand is sin management. The degree to which you have more good behavior and less bad behavior is in direct proportion to your ability to partake.

When Christians are duped into eating at this religious table, they experience the same level of anxiety, exhaustion, and disappointment as everyone else who does not use Christian language. And, as is always true at this table, the answer is simply: try harder, do more, achieve, and accumulate. It's just that the standard here is religious, and so it looks like there will be eternal benefits and blessings. Unfortunately, it is all a deception playing to the basic insecurity of not knowing who you are in Christ as God's beloved children.

The Table of the Lord

In Psalm 23, King David wrote a beautiful song that spoke of a special table. He said that this table would be for us, set in the face of our enemies. It would be a lavish table, a place of anointing and generosity, with goodness and mercy flowing in ways that none of us had seen before. This level of love would follow all who sit there every day, until they finally and forever live in the eternal Presence of God.

This table is filled with everything we will ever need, the blessings of God that bring significance, security, love, belonging, and purpose. If there were banners around this table, the messages would be life-giving words flowing from the heart of God.

- I love you.
- I choose you.
- I give you my Spirit to help you in life.
- You are welcome.

- You are wanted.
- I will be with you always.
- I crossed the universe to be with you.
- All my promises to you are yes because of Jesus.
- Come, eat freely.
- Drink until you can drink no more.
- I am preparing an eternal home for you.
- My love for you is unconditional.
- You are forgiven.
- You are free.

Sitting at the table of the Lord does not come as a reward for performance. No amount of achievement can help us. The only requirement is that we are a son or daughter of God through faith in Jesus Christ. That's it. No more than that, no less. We are welcomed and sustained by the scandalous grace of God's unconditional love.

Our seat at this table costs us nothing, but it cost Jesus everything. The One numbered among the sinners gave his life to secure our identity, bring us into union with the Father. Now, our place is set. Our strength does not qualify us, nor does our weakness disqualify us. We are there because of Jesus. We lay down all performance, power, and prestige before we come. It is inappropriate to bring such things to this table. Our hands are empty, yet open to all the Father desires to give. His giving is lavish. It is scandalous.

You will love the freedom and rest that comes from sitting at this table. It is transforming. When you are there, you will be convinced that no place could ever be better. Yet, there will be times when the lures of the evil one will entice you back. They have duped me, and most likely they will again. Why does this happen? Because there are still wounds to be healed, lies to be renounced, and losses to be grieved. We will wander and stray back to the table the world offers. But the Spirit will bring us back again, and each time we are welcomed with the Father's lavish love.

Andrei Rublev was a Russian artist who lived in the thirteenth and fourteenth centuries. He painted an icon that is now celebrated in both the eastern and western churches of the world. It is referred to as Rublev's Trinity, an exquisite painting of three heavenly beings seated at a table. These beings have come to symbolize the Father, Son, and Holy Spirit. While the portrayal, painted centuries ago, is not ethnically sensitive, it is a stunning piece of art.

A copy of this painting hangs in my office, and I meditate on it contemplatively. Not only am I drawn into the beauty of the pristine colors, and the mystical portrayal of the Trinity, I am captured by the table. On three sides sit the members of the Trinity. The fourth side of the table is open, a reminder that there is always room for me. I am invited to sit with them, to participate in this ecstatic communion, and to feast until my heart is content. I am welcomed. I am wanted. I am his child. Nothing more. Nothing less. One more thing. There is room there for you as well. Your Father waits.

For Your Reflection

1. Take a few minutes to read the story of Jesus washing the disciples' feet in John 13. What stands out to you?

2. What gave Christ the strength to do this?

3. What part did identity security play?

4. What is your understanding of the phrase, "I came to wash feet. I am not going to do less than wash feet. I am not going to do more than wash feet"?

5. Why is identity security more important than expertise?

6. In what ways do you get caught up in the emotional reactivity of others? Why?

7. How would you describe the differences between the table of the world and the table of the Lord?

8. How do some Christians try to turn the world's table into a Christian table?

9. Why is that a problem?

10. Where are you yet investing in the table of the world? Why?

11. What message is the Holy Spirit speaking into your heart at this very moment?

Notes

[1] Edwin Friedman, *Generation to Generation: Family Process in Church and Synagogue* (New York: Guilford Press, 1985, 2011), 3.

[2] Edwin Friedman, *A Failure of Nerve: Leadership in the Age of the Quick Fix* (New York: Church Publishing, 2007), 14.

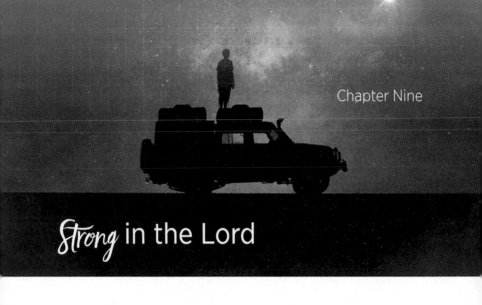

Chapter Nine

Strong in the Lord

JoAnn Ford Watson is a theologian on the faculty of Ashland Theological Seminary. She is brilliant, recognized internationally, a published author, and at times an interim Presbyterian pastor. Jody, as everyone calls her, is tireless in her service to students and their families, and she is the first to sacrifice when the demands of our institution outdistance finances and personnel. Her devotion to her elderly mother and family is the stuff of legend. Jody is one of a kind.

One more thing. JoAnn Ford Watson is possessed.

Jody has been my friend and colleague for twenty years. So when I say she is possessed, I have had a front-row seat to see her manifest this quality. You can't take her anywhere without her acting out. Everyone sees it and knows what I am talking about. I have been in the room when people see her start, look at each other, and gently shake their heads. You can't miss it about Jody. Above all other facts and accomplishments of her life it is the one characteristic that no one can miss: Jody is possessed with Christ.

Jody Watson breathes Jesus in everything she does. I have said publically that if she were pricked with a pin, Jesus would begin to leak out. If she knew I was saying this about her, she would protest energetically, in humble, self-deprecating terms. She does this because Jody doesn't see it, but everyone else does. Her life, the way she loves, her service and sacrifice exude Jesus. JoAnn Ford Watson is a person who walks the Way of Jesus the way Jesus walked the Way. I am blessed to call her friend.

The Apostle Paul was Christ possessed and was not ashamed to say so. He wrote to the Galatians saying, "I have been crucified with Christ and I no longer live, but Christ lives in me. The life I now live in the body, I live by faith in the Son of God, who loved me and gave himself for me" (2:20). Paul's security in life came through his relationship with Jesus. Christ's presence within Paul, through the Holy Spirit, had become the ground of his being, received by Paul through faith in the matchless grace of God. He wanted that fact to be crystal clear to the Galatian Christians.

Paul wrote the epistle to the Galatians because he was extremely upset that they were, in my words, wandering back to the table of the world. They had come to believe that being secure with God took faith in Christ and performance. They were teaching that obedience to the Law, rituals, and religious obligations were necessary add-ons to believing in Jesus. Their theology had become "Jesus plus performance gets you a seat at the table."

Paul was astonished. He said in no uncertain terms that they were abandoning the gospel for a message that was contrary to the good news of Christ. Getting a seat at the table does not come from performing, according to Paul, but from faith in Jesus (2:16). In fact, Paul was adamant that freedom from performance as the standard of acceptance was at the very heart of why Christ gave his life (5:1).

Paul saw identity as the foundation of union with God and the fulfillment of every core longing of our lives. That identity is "child of God." He stated that Jesus came so that we might be healed in our relationship with the Father and adopted as his children. Paul went further to say that the Holy Spirit now abides in our hearts, reminding us over and over again that God is our Abba. As a result, all that we need becomes ours through inheritance, not through performance (4:4).

Does this mean that it does not matter how we live? It means that faith in Christ secures our identity as God's children and gives us a place at the lavish table of the Lord. His scandalous grace has been poured out on us, so now we can come to his table with confidence. No performance, pleasing, or achieving needed.

Having said that, since we are now free, it is essential that we not wander back to the values and lifestyle honored at the table of the world. That would be sinful, a failure to live as who we are in Christ. The Lord knew this would not be easy, so he has given us his Spirit to help us every step of the way (5:16). Being God's child does translate into a different way of life than those who run to the world's table. We do not live a separate lifestyle in order to be accepted and secure. We do so because we are now secure as his children, possessed of Christ, and empowered by his Holy Spirit.

Strong in the Lord and the Strength of His Might

Living the Christ-possessed life is not easy. Genuinely saved people, including me, are enticed every day to compromise their identity as God's children. They wander back to the values of the world and make choices that are clearly inconsistent with the Way of Jesus. Sometimes these choices are big mistakes with huge consequences. Most of the time, the compromises are not so noticeable, but are hurtful just the same. In large and small ways, Christians end up doing very unchristian things, mostly because we forget who we are in Christ.

This world is a tough place to consistently live out of who we are as the children of God. The values of this world are shoved down our throats at every turn. We are constantly told that we are not enough and that performance, pleasing, and achieving are the keys to a successful life. These values are at the heart of all advertising, a constant barrage of promotions that tell us to do this, buy that, go here, and run there in order to be accepted and secure. Marketers are proficient at playing to our unmet needs and underlying fears. The enticement to the world's table is constant, and Christians are in no way insulated.

It is not simply the world's values that assault us, but our own weaknesses. There are more than a few parts of our lives that need to mature in Christ. Spiritual formation is a journey, and that journey takes time and a whole lot of surrender. We do not awaken to our true self through one grand existential spiritual experience. It happens as we allow the Lord to cleanse us of the debris piled up inside and as we say yes to ways in which the Holy Spirit perfects us in Jesus.

In places where we have been cleansed of wounds, lies, and losses, walking as the children of God comes easier. Where we are yet trapped in garbage, it can be tough. Our weakness makes us more susceptible to poor choices. We are more likely to allow the small-ego self to reign and rule rather than the awakened self who is free in Christ. All to say again, this is a journey.

Then, of course, there is the evil one. While Jesus has come to bring us security and the abundant life, the evil one comes as a thief to steal, kill, and destroy (John 10:10). His lures are aimed at our vulnerabilities, where deep longings remain unmet. His strategies always involve questioning the security of our identity, appealing to us with promises that core needs can be met at the table of the world. The evil one is good at hiding and infiltrating our lives through people and social systems that appear good but in the end keep us from the best. Paul said this is all-out war with the evil one, and we need to know how to recognize him and fight (Eph. 6:11–20).

Of the many things Paul said about this war against the world's values, our weakness, and the lures of Satan, one admonition stands taller for me than all the rest. He calls us to be "strong in the Lord and the strength of his might" (Eph. 6:10 RSV). Here we find two absolute essentials for living as who we are in Christ and for the awakening of our true selves. It is not enough that we know what these phrases mean. We need to experience these realities and integrate them into the way we approach life every single day.

Strong in the Lord

For too many Christians, being strong in the Lord is about theology and behavior only. While it is important that we understand basic Christian beliefs and the corresponding behaviors required of believers, knowing and doing are simply not enough. We need to experience the lavish generosity of Christ that is able to captivate our hearts and set us free to be God's awakened children. Peter prayed that we would experience grace and peace in abundance through an intimate knowing of Jesus (1 Pet. 1:2).

Nouwen wrote:

> Christian leaders cannot be persons who have well-informed opinions about the burning issues of our time. Their leadership must be rooted in the permanent, intimate relationship with the incarnate word, Jesus, and they need to find there the source for their words, advice, and guidance. . . . Leaders have to learn to listen again and again to the voice of love."[1]

What Nouwen is saying of Christian leaders must be true of all believers. We need a growing intimacy with Christ as the source of all our strength and security. This means positioning ourselves over and over again through prayer, Scripture, and other spiritual practices to meet him in the secret place deep within our lives.

Being strong in the Lord means standing on all Jesus has done for us, never compromising the gospel message that Jesus has done it all. As Paul said, "No matter how many promises God has made, they are 'Yes' in Christ" (2 Cor. 1:20). What does that mean? It means that our identity as God's children and every core longing of our lives is met because of Christ, not because of our performance.

How did you get your identity as God's child? Jesus. Will your deepest needs be met in God? Yes, because of Jesus. How do you receive forgiveness? That is Jesus also. What is the key that unlocks the Kingdom for you? Jesus. Why does the Spirit indwell your life? Jesus. Who lived a perfect life and then assigned your name to it? Jesus. How is it that you are free from condemnation? Once again, the answer is Jesus. I could go on and on with the questions, and when it comes to your standing before God, the answer is always and only Jesus.

I am captured by the litany that is included in the French Reformed liturgy of infant baptism. It reads:

Little Child, for you Jesus Christ has come, he has fought, he has suffered. For you he entered the shadow of Gethsemane and the horror of Calvary. For you he uttered the cry, "It is finished." For you he rose from the dead and ascended into heaven and there intercedes— for you, little child, even though you do not know it. But in this way the word of the Gospel becomes true. "We love him, because he first loved us."

This litany is the heart of the gospel of Christ. Notice the "for you" statements. Each represents something Jesus did for you to secure your identity and awaken your true self. Being strong in the Lord means allowing these truths of being complete in Christ to saturate every fiber of your being. It means experiencing the transforming Presence of Jesus and allowing it to empower every step you take in life. Being strong in the Lord means being Christ possessed!

Life in Christ

The following Scripture deserves our careful attention. Moving slowly through the text, pay attention to what is in bold print, for it highlights the wonder of being secure in your identity as God's child.

Therefore, **there is now no condemnation for those who are in Christ Jesus,** because through Christ Jesus the law of the Spirit who gives life has **set you free from the law of sin and death.** For what the law was power- less to do because it was weakened by the flesh, God did by sending his own Son in the likeness of sinful flesh to be a sin offering. And so he condemned sin in the flesh, in order that the **righteous requirement of the law**

might be fully met in us, who do not live according to the flesh but **according to the Spirit.**

Those who live according to the flesh have their minds set on what the flesh desires; but those who **live in accordance with the Spirit have their minds set on what the Spirit desires.** The mind governed by the flesh is death, but **the mind governed by the Spirit is life and peace.** The mind governed by the flesh is hostile to God; it does not submit to God's law, nor can it do so. Those who are in the realm of the flesh cannot please God.

You, however, are not in the realm of the flesh but **are in the realm of the Spirit, if indeed the Spirit of God lives in you**. And if anyone does not have the Spirit of Christ, they do not belong to Christ. But if Christ is in you, then even though your body is subject to death because of sin, the **Spirit gives life because of righteousness**. And if the Spirit of him who raised Jesus from the dead is living in you, **he who raised Christ from the dead will also give life to your mortal bodies** because of his Spirit who lives in you.

Therefore, brothers and sisters, we have an obligation—but it is not to the flesh, to live according to it. For if you live according to the flesh, you will die; **but if by the Spirit you put to death the misdeeds of the body, you will live.**

For those who are led by the Spirit of God are the children of God. The Spirit you received does not make you slaves, so that you live in fear again; rather, **the**

Spirit you received brought about your adoption to sonship. And **by him we cry, "Abba, Father."** The Spirit himself testifies with our spirit that we are God's children. Now **if we are children, then we are heirs**—heirs of God and co-heirs with Christ, if indeed we share in his sufferings in order that we may also share in his glory. (Rom. 8:1–17)

This Scripture is breathtaking in the way it details the difference between being God's child through faith in Christ, and living apart from Jesus through performance, pleasing, and achieving. If you are God's child, then:

- There is now no condemnation for you.
- You are set free from the law of sin and death.
- The righteous requirements of the Law have been fully met in you.
- You are able to live according to the Spirit.
- You can have your mind set on what the Spirit desires.
- Your mind can be governed by the Spirit so that you can experience life and peace.
- You can live in tune with the Spirit.
- The Holy Spirit gives life to you.
- God who raised Christ from the dead will also give life to your mortal body.
- By the Spirit you can put to death the misdeeds of the body.
- You are the child of God.
- The Spirit you received brought about your adoption.
- You get to call God "Abba, Father."
- You are not only his child, you are his heir.

Being in Christ, living as if you truly are God's child, saying yes to the awakening of your true self is what being strong in the Lord is about. It means experiencing the living Presence of Jesus in your life and feasting at the table of the Lord. No more bondage to performance and the exhausting efforts at measuring up in order to have a little dignity and respect. You are God's child, he is your Abba, and your seat at his table is forever yours. Christ possesses you, so learn to live the Christ-possessed life!

In the Strength of His Might

Albert Benjamin Simpson has been an inspiration to me, even though he died almost one hundred years ago. His life and ministry give testimony to what the Lord can do when a person surrenders their life to Christ and opens their heart to the ministry of God's power moving through human weakness. Simpson's is a legacy of global evangelism and mission, born out of a burden for the broken and his experience of God's healing Presence in his own life.

A. B. Simpson was born in Canada in the mid-nineteenth century. His passion to serve the Lord led him into pastoral ministry, first in Canada and later in Kentucky and New York City. If there ever was a person who gave his all to Christ, it was Simpson. So much so that by his late thirties he was essentially spent. His heart for Christ was huge, but it was also weakened from exhaustion. Simpson had little more to give.

A. B. went to Old Orchard Beach, Maine, for a time of rest and a spiritual camp meeting. While there, he had an encounter with the Lord that forever changed his life. Jesus told Simpson that he would like to exchange his power for Simpson's weakness. Simpson said yes, and opened his heart to the Presence and power of the Holy Spirit. Like countless others before him and after, he experienced an undefinable, yet transforming, infilling of the Holy Spirit that changed his life forever.

From that event in 1883 until his death in 1919, Simpson went on to write one hundred books and one hundred twenty hymns, to found a missionary institute that today is known as Nyack University and Alliance Theological Seminary, and to launch a denomination that today ministers Christ around the globe to millions of people. He also spearheaded a movement of physical healing that continues to this day.

Simpson was concerned that Christians everywhere understand, appreciate, and embrace the Holy Spirit. He believed that the Spirit's Presence and power are essential to effective Christian living and ministry. Over a century ago he wrote:

> We cannot leave out any part of the gospel without weakening all the rest, and if there was ever an age when the world needed the witness of God's supernatural working, it is this day of unbelief and satanic power. Therefore, we may expect as the end approaches that the Holy [Spirit] will work in healing of sickness . . . in wonderful providences . . . to prove to an unbelieving world that the power of Jesus' name is still unchanged.[2]

For Simpson the Presence of the Holy Spirit in a person's life was nonnegotiable. Simpson learned that from Jesus.

The disciples were gathered in an upper room, frightened, hiding from the religious leaders who had crucified the Lord. They had witnessed the horror of the past three days, and their emotions were on a ragged edge. Suddenly Jesus walked through the locked door! I am confident that they came close to jumping out of their skins. After Jesus essentially said, "Settle down, it's me," he did something amazing. Jesus said, "As the Father has sent me, I am sending you," and then the Bible says, "He breathed on them" (John 20:21–22).

Jesus was not huffing and puffing, out of breath from the walk up the stairs. He breathed on them intentionally. He knew the disciples needed a power far beyond themselves to accomplish the mission he gave them. So, "He breathed on them and said, 'Receive the Holy Spirit'" (v. 22). With that, Jesus was making two things crystal clear to his disciples.

First, Jesus was reminding the disciples that his ministry was completely dependent on the Presence and power of the Holy Spirit. From the moment Jesus came up out of the water of baptism, through his wilderness experience, as well as three years of preaching, teaching, and demonstrating the Kingdom of God, the Holy Spirit empowered Jesus to fulfill his mission on earth.

Second, Jesus was telling the disciples that they needed to be filled with the Holy Spirit just as he was. Jesus had already taught them that the Holy Spirit would be their Helper (John 14:16 NASB). Now, he was breathing Spirit life upon them as a reminder. It was as if he were saying, "Don't even try this on your own. You need the Helper." Days later, at the Ascension, Jesus again told them to do nothing until the Holy Spirit came upon them in power (Acts 1:4–5, 8). Ten days later the Holy Spirit fell on them, and they were never the same.

Centuries before Pentecost, God called Moses to lead his people from bondage to freedom. Moses knew that this was no small task, and in prayer asked God for help. God replied, "My Presence will go with you, and I will give you rest" (Ex. 33:14). Moses said, "If your Presence does not go with us, do not send us up from here. . . . What else will distinguish me and your people from all the other people on the face of the earth?" (33:15–16). Ever since then it has been true that the identifying mark of God's children is the Presence of the Holy Spirit upon their lives.

When Paul said that we need to be strong in the Lord, he was talking about experiencing the completed work of Christ that secures our identity as God's children. When he said we need to be strong in the strength of his might, he was talking about living in the empowerment of the Holy Spirit. Paul was making it clear that the only way to live as the children of God is through the distinguishing Presence of the Holy Spirit in our lives. This was not intended to be simply a theological point of discussion, but a daily reality of his strength made visible through our weakness.

Andrew Murray, born in 1828, was a highly educated man who spent his life in ministry in South Africa. Unbelievably, he authored two hundred forty books, many of which are seen as devotional classics to this day. One of his books is *Abide in Christ: The Joy of Being in God's Presence*. Murray believed that in knowing Jesus, we could be filled with the power that filled his life. He wrote:

> Christ gives His power in us by giving His life in us. He does not, as so many believers imagine, take the feeble life He finds in them, and impart a little strength to aid them in their feeble efforts. No; it is in giving His own life in us that He gives us His power. The Holy Spirit came down to the disciples direct from the heart of their exalted Lord, bringing down into them the glorious life of heaven which He had entered. And so His people are still taught to be strong in the Lord and in the power of His might.[3]

Murray was convinced that a disciple of Christ experiences the Holy Spirit in direct relationship to his level of expectation. He believed that a person "lives a most joyous and blessed life . . . because . . . he consents and expects to have the Mighty Savior work in him."[4]

Scripture is clear at this point: you are God's child, and you have the Holy Spirit deep within to help you realize the God-empowered potential of your true self.

For Your Reflection

1. What does it mean to be Christ possessed?

2. Why is this so important to your life?

3. What was so upsetting to Paul about the Galatian Christians adding obedience to the Law as a requirement of following Christ?

4. What is required of you to be secure as God's child?

5. What are the most significant challenges you face in living as a child of God?

6. What is the relationship between feasting at the Father's table and being strong in the Lord?

7. Review Romans 8:1–17. What stands out in this passage about what is true of you as God's child?

8. According to A. B. Simpson, what is the one thing that must never be left out of the gospel message?

9. Why must you be "strong in the strength of his might"? What does that mean to you?

10. According to Moses, what is it that distinguishes us as the people of God?

11. What did you sense the Lord saying to you while you were reading this chapter?

Notes

[1] Henri Nouwen, *In the Name of Jesus: Reflections on Christian Leadership* (New York: Crossroad, 1989), 31.

[2] A. B. Simpson, *The Holy Spirit: Vol. 2* (Harrisburg: Christian Publications), 84.

[3] Andrew Murray, *Abide in Christ: The Joy of Being in God's Presence* (Pittsburgh: Whitaker House, 1979), 182.

[4] Ibid., 183.

Chapter Ten

People Who *need* People

Unless you are deeply connected to a group of other Christians committed to the same journey, it will be impossible for you to live as a child of God and awaken to your true self. This is not a journey that can be made in isolation, and, unlike other tasks in life, on this journey surface relationships won't do. If you want to awaken to the full wonder of who you are in Christ, you must wake up to the importance of Christian community in your life and say yes to such relationships.

I am aware that the idea of deep relationships among Christians is often a frightening proposition. On one hand, people long to be known apart from any pretense. On the other, they are pretty sure that if they ever risk being real, the results will not be good. Many times I have heard believers comment on how difficult it is to choose vulnerability, particularly in church. Some have even argued that church is the last place they want to be real, because they are confident that judgment and rejection would quickly follow.

I get it. In some churches, the message that "you don't measure up" is communicated in a lot of ways, only now with serious eternal consequences. From Sunday school to sermons, people hear plenty about sin and judgment, followed by passionate admonitions to do better, work harder, and don't fall short, or else. People are aware, at least in part, of their imperfections and aren't so sure it is safe to be honest about their struggles. For some, going to church demands an application of spiritual cosmetics laid on thick to hide what is really going on in their lives. This is tragic.

I remember well a telephone call I had some years ago from a denominational executive. When he introduced himself and told me his job, I thought he was calling for some advice on church planting. I could not have been more wrong. After saying hello and engaging in the normal pleasantries, he asked if he could be honest with me. That seemed a bit strange, but I said of course, to which he said, "Please hold a moment, while I close my office door."

When he returned to the telephone, he began to cry, and through the tears he explained that he was experiencing anxiety and depression, but if this was discovered at the denominational headquarters, he would lose his job. He then proceeded to share, in depth, the struggle he was facing, and he asked if I would pray for him, which I did. This was no short conversation, and it engaged my own emotions at several points.

I knew what it was like to battle anxiety and depression. It can be debilitating and exhausting, and conquering that difficulty alone is impossible. I also experienced judgment for having an emotional struggle. He obviously was fearing the same kind of response. But most of all, I was heartbroken that he had nowhere to turn except to some author who tried to shed a little light along the path. He feared the believers he was doing life with and in essence "came by night" to someone he barely knew.

Larry Crabb wrote that the problem beneath many of our deepest struggles is a "disconnected soul."[1] He went on to define disconnection as "a condition of existence where the deepest part of who we are is vibrantly attached to no one, where we are profoundly unknown, therefore experience neither the thrill of being believed in nor the joy of loving or being loved."[2]

Disconnection at a deep soul level is to be somewhat expected when people live by the values of the world, desperately trying to measure up in order to have core longings even imperfectly met. The drive to perform demands a certain degree of hiding. Even then, however, I suspect there is a gnawing desire to be known and loved without fear of rejection or betrayal.[3]

But disconnection within the community of Christ is simply not what God wants for his people. Granted, we are imperfect and we will make mistakes. Judgment and rejection may rise up among believers, but it must be quickly replaced with the acceptance and love that God displayed in Jesus Christ, the head of the church. God is love, he sent Jesus in love, and Jesus said that love would be the one quality above all others that would identify us as his own (John 13:33–34).

Earlier I wrote that the experience of love is the emotional oxygen that nurtures the awakening of the true self. The love we need certainly flows most lavishly from God, who calls us his children. God's love must also flow from the hearts of believers toward one another. The need for one another is a sound biblical principle and must be evidenced by long-term commitments to walk the journey to awakening shoulder to shoulder, arm in arm.

Jean Vanier, a brilliant scholar and former Canadian naval officer, has proven through the L'Arche Communities he founded (now over one hundred strong globally) that there is transforming power when people belong to one another. It all began when he invited two institutionalized men with Down's syndrome to live with him in community. Since then, he has opened residential communities around the world where disabled adults find love and acceptance in the arms of caregivers who are equally transformed by the experience. Vanier writes:

> Experience has shown that one person all alone can never heal another. A one to one situation is not a good situation. It is important to bring broken people into a community of love, a place where they feel accepted and recognized in their gifts and have a sense of belonging.[4]
>
> The love and support of community gives you the certitude you are loved just as you are, with all your wounds, and that you can grow through all that. People may come to our communities because they want to serve the poor; they will only stay once they have discovered that they themselves are the poor."[5]

Community is essential to growth and healing. Connecting deeply in community is in the original DNA implanted into the people of God. We are God's children, and our God exists in community. The shared life of love and mutuality that exists eternally within the Trinity is to be reflected in the way we love, respect, and care for one another. Theologian Clark Pinnock wrote:

Fellowship on earth corresponds in measure to fellowship in heaven. The Trinity is an open, inviting fellowship, and the Spirit wants the church to be the same, responsive in the same sort of way. God wants to hear from us an echo of the dynamic relations within his own life, anticipating the coming of the kingdom. The church is meant to resemble the triune life by being itself a place of reciprocity and self-giving. The fellowship that we have with one another is related ultimately to our fellowship with the Father and Son (1 John 1:3).[6]

When we love one another well, when the qualities and characteristics of love from 1 Corinthians 13 become the characteristics of our deep connections with one another, we not only represent the coming Kingdom to a broken world, we begin to taste the not-yet of eternity in the now. When we do, that aroma of God's Kingdom beckons us to rest securely in our identity as God's eternal children. It also entices the awakening of every part of our true self hidden beneath the wounds, lies, and losses of our own imperfections.

Two Are Better Than One

The testimony of Scripture is clear about the importance of healthy relationships. Beyond the revelation that the Godhead is a community, we learn that deep connections with other people are foundational to the formative path. Consider the fact that the way God structured Israelite society highlighted interconnection. The single Israelite knew that he or she was part of a family, which was part of a clan, located within a tribe, all gathered together as the people of God.

The book of Ecclesiastes teaches us that together is far better than alone.

> Two are better than one,
> because they have a good return for their labor:
> If either of them falls down,
> one can help the other up.
> But pity anyone who falls
> and has no one to help them up.
> Also, if two lie down together,
> they will keep warm.
> But how can one keep warm alone?
> Though one may be overpowered,
> two can defend themselves.
> A cord of three strands is not quickly broken.
> (Ecclesiastes 4:9–12)

Countless stories in Scripture illustrate the importance of investing deeply in healthy relationships. Most followers of Christ have heard the stories of Moses and Aaron; Joshua and Caleb; Shadrach, Meshach, Abednego, and Daniel; Jesus and his disciples; Paul and Barnabas; and countless other supportive and formative relationships. There was power for their lives in the "and."

One of the most instructive examples of deep connection comes from the story of David and Jonathan, found in the book of 1 Samuel. The Bible makes it clear that their hearts were knit together through shared experiences and trials. Close communion as friends deeply shaped their lives, impacting the choices they would make during extremely difficult times. At one point, David and Jonathan made a covenant of love and commitment that went soul deep (20:17). That connection of unconditional love had profound implications for their own growth and development as men of God.

When most Christians hear the word *soul*, they think it refers to the spiritual part of their lives that goes to heaven when they die. That is a narrow understanding of what is a vast and multifaceted aspect of being human. The soul encompasses every dimension of life: spirit, heart, mind, thoughts, feelings, actions, relationships, and virtually everything it means to be human. In countless ways throughout every day, God, through the Holy Spirit, is seeking to form the soul, unleashing the full potential of what it means for us to be redeemed in Christ and reflect the image of God as sons and daughters.

The relationships we choose impact the development of our lives, or better said, the shape of our souls. Spiritual formation happens in many ways, not the least of which is the nature of the connections we have with other people. The quality of the connections we make with others impacts us profoundly, forming the character of our lives. This is serious business. It is why we need to surround ourselves with Christians who are surrendering to the Holy Spirit as he shapes their lives to reflect the nature of Christ. So you and I must take the nature and quality of our relationships seriously. Healthy connections shape our souls. They are also the context in which Jesus engages us most deeply.

A Gathering of Two or Three

Jesus Christ said long ago that he would be present where two or three gather in his name (Matt. 18:20). "In his name" means that we come together centered in Christ, reflecting that we are Christ possessed in the way we love one another. The quality of the love he has demonstrated toward us is then the very nature of the love we extend to one another. Every time we connect at that depth, we all the more awaken to who we are as God's children. We move beyond being individuals who simply share a common faith in Christ. We become his forever family.

Vanier writes:

> More and more people are becoming conscious that our God is not just a powerful Lord telling us to obey or be punished, but our God is *family.* Our God is three persons in love with each other; our God is communion. And this beautiful and loving God is calling us humans into this life of love. We are not alone; we are called together to drop barriers, to become vulnerable, to become one. The greatest thirst of God is that "they may be one, perfectly one, totally one." But we have to die to all the powers of egoism in ourselves in order to be reborn for this new and deeper unity where our uniqueness and personal gifts and creativity are not crushed, but enlivened and enhanced.[7]

This type of community does not come easily. It takes time and more than a few bumps along the way. When our "stuff" is welcomed out of hiding, patience and love are required in heavy doses. There are times when it is easier to love people in prayer rather than face to face. If we take the risks, however, we will never want to walk this journey alone again. Community becomes the dwelling place of the Spirit, and where the Spirit is present, the Kingdom of God becomes manifest in our midst.

Vulnerability requires that I tell you that community was not my first choice. I was wounded by people, mostly church people, and wanted little to do with being open about my brokenness.

God's severe mercy, however, placed me in a season where I had to be open. In the strangest of places, a psychiatric hospital, I connected with some Christ followers who did not have the energy to pretend and who, out of desperation, stood shoulder to shoulder in darkness and said, "Let's walk this out together."

That experience transformed my thinking. Ever since then, I have had the pleasure of walking this journey with deeply committed, certainly imperfect, yet amazingly wonderful men and women of different ages, theologies, ethnicities, and wounding. We share a common Father, have developed a common language of healing, and voice a common desire to live secure as the children of God, awakening to all God created us to be. We come together regularly from places across the country and around the globe. Yet no matter how long we have been apart or how different our experiences, we connect as family and we are being changed.

Science Weighs In

The Lord has allowed me the opportunity to equip Christian caregivers in a modality of emotional healing that centers in Jesus Christ. I chose to call this method formational prayer, a ministry of the Holy Spirit moving through a Christian caregiver in order to position a broken person to experience the healing Presence of Jesus Christ. Over the past two decades I have written several books on this topic and have had well over six thousand caregivers, counselors, pastors, psychologists, and physicians attend different seminars and advanced classes.

I have seen many people experience deep emotional and physical healing as they were positioned by the Lord to journey into their own broken pasts to reclaim what was abused and taken. I have had a front-row seat to the love of God pouring out into the hearts of people who were in bondage. It has been amazing and humbling, to say the least. I would love to share specific stories here, but if you are interested in them, you will need to look at some of my other books.

I do want to share, however, that in formational prayer I seek to integrate a biblical foundation, sound theology, and insights from the behavioral sciences. I am convinced that an intersection of these three bodies of knowledge provides a powerful space for personal transformation. Of course, added to that, we work to position people to actually engage the Spirit of Christ in a healing experience that sets them free.

I have been especially interested and somewhat moved to discover that behavioral science shares the Lord's belief that community matters. No, I am not saying that science consistently recognizes that Jesus knew long ago what science has now caught up to believe. But belief in the power of community has become a cornerstone of what the behavioral sciences believe to be necessary for psychological and emotional well-being.

Renowned scientist and psychiatrist Daniel Siegel writes that:

> The brain is genetically programmed to be social. . . . In fact, the brain is hardwired to take in signals from the social environment to alter its own internal states. Our minds emerge from this interdependence of the brain and interpersonal relationships. . . . Finding meaning in belonging emerges as we join with a process much larger than our individual skin-defined lives.[8]

Christian psychiatrist and author Curt Thompson addresses the impact of relationships in his book *The Soul of Shame: Retelling the Stories We Believe about Ourselves.* Expanding on Siegel's work on the nature of the mind, Thompson has concluded:

> From the day we enter the world, our neurons are firing not only from the depths of genetically influenced patterns, but also in response to the myriad of social interactions we sense and perceive when we encounter other people. . . . In this way, our relational interactions can actually influence our lives at the most basic biological level.[9]

Thompson's attention in his recent book is on the power of shame that arises at least in part from a person's inherent sense that they simply do not measure up. He goes on to suggest that the journey to the healing of shame must be taken with other people where we, and our stories, can be known in the deepest sense of that word. This demands an openness and vulnerability that reflects the heart of God for his beloved children.[10]

But Who Gets Past the Gate?

It should be clear by now that Christians are called to journey in life connected to other people. We have seen that community is the nature of our triune God. It is a foundational biblical principle taught and modeled by Christ, and it is now proven to be essential to psychological development and emotional healing. We people need people. But we also need discernment and wisdom regarding the characteristics and qualities of those we allow access to the deepest part of our lives.

Yes, we are to love people everywhere. That is a fundamental teaching of our Lord. However, loving people does not mean that everyone is safe enough, or mature enough, to honor and respect us as children of God or to contribute to the awakening of our true selves. We must learn to be quite careful about who we let in to help us in our own journey to freedom. While all people deserve respect and dignity, not everyone should be permitted to speak into our lives.

I want to revisit a metaphor I used in a previous resource to help you understand the characteristics of personal identity. It may also inform you as to the nature of healthy personal growth, with particular attention to who you allow to help you in identity development. [11]

A ranch can serve as a helpful metaphor for your life. It illustrates the need to exercise proper care and concern, as well as the importance of setting boundaries with people. What is within the ranch represents the various gifts and endowments that are part of what makes you healthy and unique. The care and development of every part of the ranch is your responsibility. You may need help along the way, but the condition of your ranch is determined by the attention you give to personal growth. No one else has that responsibility. It is yours.

The following illustration provides a visual representation of the ranch concept. Notice the particular parts of the ranch.

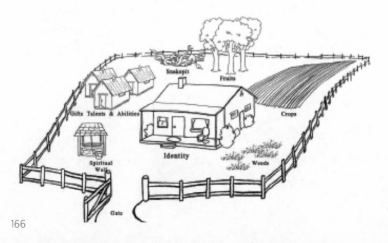

On your ranch are several buildings that are essential for your personal health and well-being. First, there is a main house, which in this allegory represents your identity, that is to be securely founded upon the certainty that you are God's beloved child. You are loved, cherished, and accepted by him, fully pleasing and embraced through the righteousness of the Lord Jesus Christ. This rich endowment is given freely by the God of Love. Growing in understanding and confidence in your identity is the way you maintain the main structure of this ranch. The world works hard to convince you that success, money, popularity, and power define you. But when your main house is built on Christ, there is nothing more to earn or prove.

Also on this ranch is a well; it is the place where Living Water is supplied. It is important that you keep this well maintained and clear so that the water will always flow, pure and refreshing. Prayer, Scripture reading, and communion with the Lord are to be a daily part of your life, providing regular access to the stream of the Lord. Water is the difference between life and death, so guarding and developing this part of your ranch is essential.

You may notice some outbuildings on your ranch. These represent unique storehouses that hold those qualities that make you special and unique. Like sheds that shelter the tractors and machinery that keep a ranch productive and well-maintained, these outbuildings are storehouses for your spiritual gifts, special talents, and particular skills. They also store your attitudes, appetites, personality traits, and preferences. Whenever needed, you choose the appropriate resource and employ it with maturity and satisfaction.

There is an orchard on your ranch, where the fruits of the Spirit are nurtured and developed. There are fields, where a harvest of righteousness is cultivated and, in season, gathered to the glory of the Lord. The produce of these fields will sustain you, as well as providing others with nourishment and help when they are in special need.

Because you live in a fallen world and will wander into sin, there are weedbeds on the ranch, places within that need to be brought under control through the Holy Spirit. You must not turn a blind eye to such unsightly places. You should lean into the Lord for help in bringing that part of the ranch in line with his Word. And, of course, there would be the occasional snakepit, where lingering and counter-productive habits dwell, in need of Christ's cleansing touch. Such places are often well out of sight, hidden from view in the dark recesses of past wounding, lies, and losses. You will want to be especially diligent in asking the Lord to help you remove them from your life.

Finally, your metaphorical ranch has a gate. You are responsible to determine who is allowed to enter your ranch, and who would be politely, yet definitively, kept outside. Don't be confused at this point. The ranch represents your identity and inner life. The only reason a person should enter would be to help you develop or maintain some aspect of your well-being. Anyone invited to help would only have access to that part of the ranch that you feel safe to entrust to their care and instruction. This helping person would stay only as long as the caregiver felt necessary.

For example, if you were finding it difficult to maintain the well of your spiritual life, you might want to invite someone through the gate and onto your ranch who could help do that. Possibly this person could give insights and suggestions about prayer or some other spiritual discipline. They would not be able to make the changes or to force you to do anything, for the well is your responsibility. The helping person could give suggestions and direction that would equip you to find a better flow of living water. Once a person completed the desired task, he or she would step outside the gate to meet and relate with you in the normal discourse of life.

Anyone who, through words or actions, would intentionally or unintentionally compromise the main house of your identity, or poison the well of your spirituality, or try to force his or her will upon you is unsafe and should not be permitted to enter. That does not mean that you would be unkind or unfriendly. You can and should be kind, generous, and caring, and socialize with all people. But unsafe people should not have access to negatively impact the security of your identity, or to mess with the precious endowments that bring growth and safety to your life. There is no good or legitimate reason for you to blindly open the gate to just any person's influence. Your inner life belongs to you, and you decide who comes through the main gate to help you live, based on your true identity as God's child.

No one has the right to force his or her way onto your ranch and insist that you think, act, or behave in a certain way. Nor is anyone free to barge in and redefine who you are, how you feel, or what you believe. The fence is the boundary, and you alone are responsible for what happens on your ranch. It is your right and responsibility to develop and maintain every aspect of your property. No one else has the responsibility to make your ranch productive, nor do they have the right to come barging in and do whatever they may please. The fence represents your boundaries and is there to limit access to your ranch. The gate is where you wisely determine if someone has honorable intentions and is there to help.

In a perfect world, you would have learned about ranching (taking responsibility for your identity and inner life) from your parents. At birth, knowing that you were a helpless child, they would have protected and nurtured your ranch. With God's guidance, they would have set the fence in place to keep you from harm and laid a foundation for the main house by praying and speaking the identity of Christ into your life. They would have started to establish the well of your relationship with Christ, and so forth. As you grew, they would have taught you how to develop and maintain your own ranch. At first they would have invited you to watch them care for your ranch. As you grew, they would ask you to help, as a way of learning. Eventually, your parents would step back to watch you care for yourself, making sure that you understood the essentials of ranching. When confident that you were old enough and mature enough to care for your ranch, they would lovingly exit the ranch, giving full responsibility to you.

People at the Gate

One of the most important responsibilities you have regarding your own ranch (your deep inner life) is deciding who to allow past the front gate. Remember, normal socialization takes place outside the gate. That is where you connect with people, extend love, generosity, grace, and care. Allowing someone to step through the gate represents permitting someone to shape who you are as a person. Unfortunately, many of us have allowed unsafe people to have a deep impact on our sense of self, our spiritual life, the development and use of our gifts, and more. In many cases, we did not even know it was permissible, let alone essential, that we not give them access.

Recently I was doing a seminar in which I was talking about not allowing unsafe people open access to determine or change our identity. I said that we have the right to establish boundaries with people. I also emphasized that we must be discerning about when and who we allow to shape our sense of self. More than a few participants were stirred by my comments and felt it was somehow unchristian to set boundaries to keep out unsafe people. One woman went so far as to say, "The person who wounds me the most is my mother. It would be wrong, wouldn't it, to not let her say and do what she does?"

That hits right at the core of one of our greatest needs regarding community. Who do we let in to mold our inner life and shape the way we live out our identity as God's child? Conversely, who should we keep at the gate and not permit to impact our sense of self with their words and actions? These are critical questions. Community is essential for the journey, but we must be keenly discerning regarding who connects with the deepest part of who we are as God's child.

The Holy Spirit needs to give us wisdom and maturity on this matter. We cannot isolate ourselves. We need one another in order to be spiritually formed. It is equally essential that we are discerning. Not everyone in our lives is safe. A little thought and awareness might reveal that some people deserve our love but not necessarily our complete trust. I want to give some insight on who might better stay at the gate and who should be welcomed to help us live up to who we are in Christ and to awaken us as God's chosen children.

Those who stay outside the gate—any persons who seek to:

- *Dominate*—People who violate your boundaries and insist on controlling who you are, what you do, and who you will become.
- *Manipulate*—People who use cunning and shame to get you to choose and respond according to their desires.

- *Triangulate*—People who try to draw you into the middle of conflicts with other people and try to get you to take responsibility for what they refuse to do.
- *Instigate*—People who stir up negative feelings through criticism and unhelpful comments about some aspect of your life.
- *Suffocate*—People who refuse to allow you room to grow in your own way and time, and who demand that love is best expressed by allowing them to micromanage your life.
- *Humiliate*—People who work through words and actions to make you look small and insignificant in an area, communicating that you simply do not measure up.
- *Violate*—People who abuse you in any way and to even the smallest degree, be that physically, sexually, emotionally, relationally, or spiritually.
- *Interrogate*—People who want close to you simply to get information they can use against you or others, or to be more important in the eyes of other people.

These eight trespassers stay at the gate! You can love them, respect them as people, care about them, and be with them in community. But they must not be permitted to use words and actions to impact your inner life and sense of self.

What follows is a list of people you might welcome to help you on the inner journey. Unlike the eight who must stay at the gate, these people are full of characteristics that will help you grow in the wonder of who you are in Christ. People who are:

- *Worship-full*—People who are Christ possessed, who live lives that bring glory to the Father, and who have met him on their own journey of descent.

- *Respect-full*—People who treat you as the child of God you are, who celebrate your dignity and honor your boundaries.
- *Grace-full*—People who have experienced the scandalous grace of Christ and now extend the grace-saturated embrace to you as his beloved one.
- *Resource-full*—People who have grown and matured through their own inner journey and have knowledge and abilities specific to the areas where you need help.
- *Care-full*—People who embody the love of God, who are generous in their approach to you and able to connect to you with deep empathy and understanding.
- *Insight-full*—People who are seasoned on the journey and, through success and failure, have gained wisdom that will help you awaken to the person God created you to be in him.
- *Faith-full*—People who trust the providence of God and have surrendered their lives to both his care and his will for their lives.
- *Grate-full*—People who are quick to give thanks to God for all he has provided as their Father, and who express that gratitude through a life of generosity and blessing.

Jesus did not walk through his life and ministry alone. Neither should we. The Lord had different levels of relationships, from the crowds that listened to him, to the seventy that he taught to minister to the Kingdom, to the twelve who were his closest friends, to the three he asked to stay at his side in Gethsemane. Our lives should be much the same. People should matter to us, and different types of relationships should bring a richness to our days. And yet, there are those few whom we will allow to draw close. Who might those people be for you?

For Your Reflection

1. What feelings arise in you when you read that connecting with other people is essential for the journey to freedom?

2. Why is community such a foundational principle of Christianity?

3. What did Larry Crabb mean by "disconnection"?

4. What problems arise when a person experiences disconnection?

5. Why are some people afraid to be vulnerable in church?

6. What are your thoughts regarding Siegel's and Thompson's insights on the importance of community for brain development?

7. Why is vulnerability so important to experiencing freedom as a child of God?

8. According to the ranch metaphor, what are the components of your inner life?

9. Who is responsible for your deep internal development as a child of God?

10. What role does the Holy Spirit play in that development?

11. Are you allowing access to any of the eight who should stay at the gate?

12. What will you do about this?

13. Make a list of people you know who share the "full" characteristics listed in this chapter.

14. What first steps toward healthy connections is the Lord asking you to make?

Notes

[1] Larry Crabb, *Connecting: A Radical New Vision* (Nashville: Word, 1997), *xvi*.

[2] Ibid., 44.

[3] Gilbert Bilezikian, *Community 101:Reclaiming the Local Church as a Community of Onenness* (Grand Rapids: Zondervan, 1997), 15.

[4] Jean Vanier, *From Brokenness to Community* (Mahwah, NJ: Paulist Press, 1992), 28.

[5] Ibid., 20.

[6] Pinnock, *Flame of Love,* 117 (see chap. 5, n. 1).

[7] Vanier, *Brokenness to Community,* 35

[8] Daniel J. Siegel, "An Interpersonal Neurobiology of Psychotherapy: The Developing Mind and the Resolution of Trauma," in *Healing Trauma: Attachment, Mind, Body, and the Brain,* ed. Marion Solomon and Daniel Siegel (New York: W. W. Norton, 2003), 7.

[9] Curt Thompson, *The Soul of Shame: Retelling the Stories We Believe about Ourselves* (Downers Grove: IVP Books, 2015), 40.

[10] Ibid., 14.

[11] This section is adapted from my book *Healing Care, Healing Prayer: Helping the Broken Find Wholeness in Christ* (Abilene, TX: Leafwood, 2001), 53–57.

Chapter Eleven

Final *Thoughts*

Darren introduced himself on the final day of the Identity Integrity and the Awakening of the True Self seminar. He was deeply touched by what took place and wanted to thank me. I could see joy on his face. It was clear that the Lord had touched Darren, which is always the greatest outcome of any time I stand before people and talk about Jesus. It is the Presence of Jesus, through the Spirit, that brings transformation, and Darren had encountered him in a powerful way.

Darren shared a bit of his story with me. He had not been in church or in a Christian gathering for over twenty-five years. Darren had wandered away from the Lord in his mid-thirties and had made choices that were far more in line with the table of the world than with his inheritance as a child of God. He had been living with a woman for almost a decade but never had felt the need to get married to her. Darren said that other lifestyle choices were "probably not want God would want."

A close friend who served on my staff had invited Darren, or, as he said, "kept bugging him about showing up." I smiled when he told me that, and asked, "Well, what do you think?" Tears welled up in his eyes, and Darren told me that the four days at the seminar were like coming home. He was deeply moved by what he experienced and said that it was exactly what he needed, even though he didn't know he needed it before he came. He said that he felt better and, again, wanted to say thanks.

I felt led to press Darren a bit, so I asked him a pointed question. "Darren, do you see this experience as a vacation from your normal life, or an invitation to a new way of life?" He was not sure what I was suggesting, so I went on. "You have had an experience with Jesus, and that is great. But being secure in your identity as God's child is an invitation to a journey, not a one-time spiritual experience. You have a decision to make. Were these four days simply a time away or a call to a new way of life?" Darren looked at me for a long minute and then said, "I see what you are talking about. I'll need to think about that."

This matter of saying yes, of living as the child of God and experiencing the awakening of your true self, is serious business. For many, like Darren, it means turning away from the way of the world in some practical ways. It involves laying down what is not of the Lord in our lives and making room for Jesus. The biblical word for this is frightening to some, but it involves making some first steps in Christ's direction. It involves repentance.

Repentance conjures up all kinds of images for people. Unfortunately, most of them are negative. It actually means making practical steps to turn into the Way of Jesus. If we are his followers, then that is what we want at the deepest level of who we are. Our true self desires to make that turn, and it brings us onto the path that leads to greater security and freedom as God's child.

Major W. Ian Thomas was a British officer during World War II. He was a man of great faith and intimacy with the Lord. Following his service in the armed forces, he founded Capenwray Missionary Fellowship Torchbearers, which today provides many conference centers and Bible schools around the world.

Major Thomas lived his life believing and teaching that Christ alive in you is the key to experiencing the abundant life. He authored numerous books focusing on that theme. Today they are recognized around the world as Christian classics. In his book *The Indwelling Life of Christ,* he defined repentance. He wrote:

> True repentance is not being sorry for something you have done wrong. No, if you do something wrong, you *should* be sorry; but that is not real repentance.
>
> Real repentance is hilariously exciting. It is facing the facts of life, recognizing how God made you, how you were intended to function, and then being restored to that relationship of mutual interavailability that the Lord Jesus enjoyed between Himself and the father, a mutual interavailability in which you are prepared to let Him be God. That is true repentance.[1]

True repentance is the way we position ourselves before God so that he has complete access to our lives. It involves our practical next steps that give room for the Lord to do what we could never do for ourselves. What follows is a brief discussion of what some of those next steps might look like for you and for any of us who want to go deeper with the Lord and live free as his awakened children.

Take Responsibility for Your Journey

Earlier the discussion focused on the debris that builds up in our lives and keeps us from being free. Specifically I highlighted the presence of sin, wounds, lies, and loss. Each of these has a devastating impact on our lives and must be cleansed if we hope to experience freedom. This aspect of the journey involves a level of awareness and examination, led by the Holy Spirit. It also demands a posture of surrender, where the Lord purges us of what is not like him in order to release who we truly are as God's children. As I warned, this journey of descent takes time and patience.

When it comes to the sins we commit—those dysfunctional behaviors that are more of the world than the Lord, we understand responsibility. We did it. We made the choices. We must take responsibility and confess before the Lord and seek his cleansing. "The devil made me do it" really is no excuse, even when he threw out the lure that caught us. I believe we know this, so we hold fast to the promise of 1 John 1:9 that if we confess our sins, the Lord will both forgive and purify us.

But what about wounds, lies, and loss? In many cases, these occur in our lives at the hands of others. Such things are clearly not our fault, especially when we have been the victims of other people's bad behavior. While it is true that these damages are not our fault, dealing with them is still our responsibility. We must seek the Lord's healing and cleansing. We cannot and must not wait for the people who wounded us to come and make things right. That gives them far too much power.

The journey to live as God's beloved child is your responsibility. You must say yes to his transforming work. No one can or should be responsible to say yes for you. There is no doubt that only the

Lord can bring deep change to your life. That is clearly his part of the journey. But it is yours and only yours to surrender and say yes.

Be Strong in the Lord

Ian Thomas once wrote that there was nothing as boring as Christianity without Christ.[2] I could not agree more. Without the Presence of Christ in our midst, Christianity becomes, practically, little more than another religion based on human effort. It is based on performance and prioritizes obedience to rules and religious obligations. There is no life without Jesus.

There is life, however, and that life is in Jesus. Paul said that the glorious riches of God's mystery is "Christ in you, the hope of glory" (Col. 1:27), Christ who lives inside of you, the One who made it so that your identity is secure as Abba's child (Gal. 4:4), who made you alive, forgave your sins, cancelled the charge owed by you, and disarmed every power and authority aligned against you (Col. 2:11–15), and who made every promise of God yes to us who are his children (2 Cor. 1:20).

You must never allow yourself to believe that you are required to add to what Christ did. That is the lie propagated at the table of the world. Be strong in the Lord, give thanks moment by moment for all he has accomplished, and meditate on the wonder of Jesus alive in you. A practical next step is to spend time with your Bible, reading the Gospels, and thinking deeply of what Paul says about Jesus in you. It will take your breath away. You will, like Paul, become Christ crazy.

Major Thomas wrote:

I know of nothing so utterly exciting as being a
Christian, sharing the very Life of Jesus Christ on earth

right here and now, caught up with Him into relentless, invincible purposes of the almighty God, and having available to us all the limitless resources of Deity for accomplishing those purposes.

Can you imagine anything more exciting than that?[3]

Lean into the Holy Spirit

In two epistles the Apostle Paul wrote that the Holy Spirit dwells inside us, reminds us continuously that we are Abba's child, and is there to help us walk in freedom (Rom. 8:16 and Gal. 4:4). This makes the Holy Spirit a most important guest, so each of us must learn to be a welcoming host!

We must not allow the Holy Spirit to become little more than a theological concept and discussion point. The Holy Spirit is God with us, animating our lives so that we can walk the Way of Jesus just as he did. Jesus referred to him as the Paraclete, which in Greek is actually *parakletos,* the one who will "stand alongside" us when we need him. In this case, he is not only alongside, he is *inside*, empowering each of us as God's beloved and chosen child.

Granted, the Holy Spirit is more than a bit mysterious. For some people, because of the way he has been portrayed, he can seem downright frightening. Jesus himself said that "the wind blows wherever it pleases. You hear its sound, but you cannot tell where it comes from or where it is going. So it is with everyone born of the Spirit" (John 3:8). The Holy Spirit can be uncontrollable, undeniable, and unpredictable. Yet he is, according to Jesus, the Comforter who stands with us.

When you were born again, it was the Holy Spirit who awakened you and gave you a new heart (John 3:3–8; Ezek. 36:26–27). Ever since the Holy Spirit came to live inside you, he has worked to align your life with the way of Jesus. He sets you free from what once held you in bondage, so that you can now live as who you truly are in Christ (Rom. 8:14–17). It is the Holy Spirit who poured out special graces (spiritual gifts) on your life. He did this so that you will uniquely contribute to the movement of God's Kingdom reign here on earth (1 Cor. 12).

The Holy Spirit also desires to empower you with his Presence. That is what happened to the disciples in Acts 2, and Paul has promised that this infilling Presence is available to you over and over again (Eph. 5:18). The Holy Spirit is God's gift that keeps on giving to you. I encourage you to learn more of the Spirit in the New Testament, gather with other believers who experience his Presence, and open your heart to the power that only he can bring to your life as God's beloved.

Learn to Abide

An interesting and telling story forms the heart of the book of Haggai. The children of Israel returned from captivity to find Jerusalem in ruins. Worst of all, the Temple had been completely destroyed. God promised his blessings, and they began to rebuild the Lord's house. They laid the foundation and set up the altar and began to make sacrifices before the Lord. After that, they turned to building their own homes, intending to get back to the Temple and finish rebuilding it. A long time passed, and they were still distracted by their own wants.

God sent his prophet named Haggai to shake things up. He told the people to examine their lives. He asked them, "Is it a time for you yourselves to be living in your paneled houses while this house remains a ruin?" (1:4). Haggai then pointed out that avoiding building the house of God had led to their own poverty, and he admonished them to get their priorities straight and build the house of God (1:5–11).

There is an important lesson here. We must take time to invest in our relationship with the Lord. Jesus used the metaphor of a vine and branches (John 15:1–17). While he first called you to follow him, he then invited you to abide with him. He wants a deep connection with you, and he promises that if you remain in him, you will live a fruitful life characterized by joy (15:11). Jesus goes on to teach that abiding in him will lead to a deep relationship with the Father, particularly in the effectiveness of your prayer life (15:16).

What does abiding involve? I suggest the following.

- *It is relational and not transactional.* It is an invitation to come close to the Lord as Mary did, present to the One who loves you deeply as God's child (Luke 10:38–42).
- *You must eliminate in order to concentrate.* Pruning means eliminating what is not in the flow of the Lord's Presence and power in your life. If you wonder what that might be, ask the Spirit.
- *It is about positioning, not performing.* Choose to engage spiritual disciplines and spiritual exercises as a way of encountering the Lord and being changed in his Presence. Doing this is not a way of measuring up!
- *You lay down life to find life.* No more chasing after the table of the world, but instead learn to rest in your position as God's child. Feast on Christ through worship and prayer.
- *Watch new fruit grow.* You will experience new life and excitement as you abide in Christ. No more striving when you learn abiding.

Move from Mastery to Mystery

The message that you do not measure up, that you are not enough to deserve respect and dignity as you are, led you to develop the small-ego self. You did this to control and respond to your world. It was the only way you knew to protect yourself and to try to satisfy your deepest longings. It is what you were taught and what you caught as you watched the world around you.

Mastery is an increasingly sophisticated effort to find security and significance through performance, pleasing, accumulating, and achievement. Gifts, talents, abilities, and passions are used in an attempt to get to the world's table and find some satisfaction. Mastery is transactional, and demands competency in the rules, rites, rituals, and obligations that promise meaning.

With mastery, life is a scoreboard, and you are obligated to compare and compete. The world promotes the notion that there are A players and B players, and the As have it all. As such, mastery demands investments in power, prestige, and possessions. The lure promises life, but once in your grasp, it always brings brokenness and death.

The journey to self-awakening and identity security is far more mystery than mastery. Difficulty and disappointment open the door to a new journey; crises challenge you to relinquish to God who you are and to be free. You are invited to put away childish things and awaken to the transforming power of love that brings you into union with your Father (1 Cor. 13:11).

Embracing the mystery does evoke some fear. There are no formulas and rules to guide you, except the law of love. You become less sure in yourself, and yet more convinced of Christ and the Presence of the Holy Spirit. You know he is the wind that blows where he will, but in mystery the center by which you navigate will be Jesus: his life and his teachings.

Mystery is relational, a call to union with the Father. In him you find security, the assurance that you are now and will forever be his child. In mystery you lay down performance, and giving it up opens the way to transformation. Information alone never satisfies in mystery, only the Presence of the Lord that changes you in the deepest part of who you are.

The values in mystery are different than those in mastery. Pretense is replaced with vulnerability, activity with stillness, power is laid down for weakness, and the only way to conquer is through surrender. It all appears upside down, and yet the ground beneath your feet will never feel more solid. Mystery is where the true self abides, in the present moment—the now of God's abundant Presence. And love, which we identified earlier as the emotional oxygen that nurtures your true self, will indeed flow to and through your life.

Connect Deeply

It is essential that you connect with people who share the journey toward identity security and the awakening of the true self. There is something transformational though mysterious about joining with people who are passionate about Christ and vulnerable about their own need for healing and freedom. Honesty, humility, and the Father's love create a special bond between those who say yes to this sacred path. The tension between weakness and strength, mentioned by Paul in 2 Corinthians 12:9–10, holds great hope for those who walk this path shoulder to shoulder.

I highly recommend two connections. They have been formational in my life, and I am convinced they will be for you. First, find a qualified and gifted spiritual director. Spiritual direction is best defined as helping others discover God's movement in life and encouraging them to respond appropriately. A spiritual director helps you increase your awareness of God's activity in your life. He or she also introduces spiritual exercises that help connect you with the Lord's Presence and power.

A spiritual director, or spiritual guide if you prefer, can be a Christian brother or sister who is more mature and seasoned on the journey. He or she can also be a person who has received special education in the history and practice of spiritual direction. Such training is more common these days. One organization that provides such training and help is HCM International. They have an easily accessible website that provides names of endorsed spiritual directors who are Christ centered and familiar with the journey to freedom in Christ.

I also recommend that you consider finding someone who can pray with you about the debris of wounds, lies, and loss in your life. I have developed a way, though by far not the only way, to position people for emotional healing called formational prayer. I have written about this approach in several books, most specifically in *Healing Care, Healing Prayer* and *Strong Winds, Crashing Waves*. Many people around the world have been trained in this ministry. Connecting with HCM International would be a good first step to finding help.

Regardless of the specific training someone might have, do pray about finding help. A spiritual director or formational caregiver might be a great step to deeper healing and freedom.

Resist the Lure of the World's Table

All Christians, to one degree or another, are investing in the world's table. We are broken people who are susceptible to the lures of the evil one. Even when our hearts' desire is to live awakened and secure to who we are as God's children, core longings can be easy prey for the strategies of darkness.

I have been grateful for the patience the Lord has shown me on my journey to freedom. I find that I can be maturing in one area, by his grace, yet far from choosing his best in another. That is the nature of the journey and why we will not reach perfection until we see him face to face. This is not a quick fix. Anyone enamored by instant cash, instant-on television, and instant Internet connections may become frustrated, because spiritual formation is not a moment-in-time experience.

Ask the Lord to show you where he most wants you to turn from the table of the world to security in him. Ask the Holy Spirit to enlighten you to that one area where he is working right now in your life. Recently, I became aware that I was investing too deeply in my career as the foundation of significance. I was initially blind to what I was doing, but surrender and relinquishment opened my eyes, and I saw, even though it was uncomfortable, that I had wandered.

A possible practical strategy would be to:

- Ask the Lord where you are investing in the world's table for core-longing needs.
- Once your eyes are open, seek the Spirit's help in uncovering what this has cost you as a child of God.
- Let the Lord take you deeper to the wound, or lie, or loss that may be driving this choice.
- Invite God to begin cleansing that debris and to disconnect you from the lure the evil one has placed before you.

- Watch for circumstances that arise that entice you back to that table relative to that area of your life.
- Ask the Spirit to help you choose according to your identity as his child.

Seek a New Vision

One day as I was meditating in prayer, I sensed the Lord asking a rather surprising question of me. "Terry, what do you want to be true of you when your strength has failed?" What the Lord was asking was not clear to me. I was healthy and, all things being equal, anticipated years ahead of me. I asked the Lord to clarify the question, and he gave me a mental picture of myself years from now, stooped over, white hair, clearly an elderly man. With that, I understood.

What do I hope is true when I am near the end of a long life? I would desire to be ending well, full of faith and courage. I would hope that my intimacy with the Lord had deepened substantially, and that my confidence in Jesus was unwavering. I would want to be Christ possessed, and for sure truly living as God's beloved child. I would want to see that, like my Lord, I chose to serve far more than be served, to be a blessing flowing from the blessings I had received.

What came next from the Lord was just as startling, yet crystal clear. "Invest in becoming that man every day, beginning right now." Ending well doesn't just happen. Finishing well begins now, with each choice I make, every investment in my spiritual formation, and all the steps ahead on the journey. I will not walk this path perfectly, and I am sure I will stumble along the way. But the end should be always in mind. "What do you want to be true of your life when strength has failed you?" Ask the Lord. I am sure he will show you.

There is, finally, a critical aspect of the life well-lived. It is both taught and modeled by our Lord. Jesus was secure in his identity as the Father's Son, thus he was able to lay down his life for others. Knowing who he was, where he came from, and where he was going, the Lord chose to serve rather than be served (John 13:1–17). He never used his power to his own advantage. Instead he became a servant so that broken people would be healed and set free (Phil. 2:6–7). Jesus laid down his life as an act of love, and then he encouraged us to do the same (1 John 3:16; John 15:13).

Embracing the sacramental life, becoming a channel of God's love, means more than dying well, though that is certainly part of it. It involves living well as a person who serves the Kingdom by caring for the broken, outcast, lost, and imprisoned. It is characterized by moving from a "what's in it for me" mentality, to "what can I do for others" in Jesus's name.

We live in a self-centered culture that seems to prioritize me and mine. Sometimes that attitude leaks into the church, giving the impression that coming to Christ is all about how being a Christian benefits "my" life, now and forever. Certainly there are those benefits, but in the end a person secure in their identity as a son or daughter of God embraces a radically different view of life. Ending well—the life well-lived—is more than being blessed. It is about being a blessing, a faithful steward of the rich resources of the Kingdom the Father gives to his children.

Praise be to the Father, you are his beloved, chosen, and empowered child. Christ Jesus came to bring you into the arms of the One who loves you with an everlasting love. That love has, is, and will nurture you to the fullness of your identity. His love will satisfy your deepest longings, pour out into service to others, and bring you safely into his eternal embrace. How do I know this is true of you? Because God's word says it is so.

> *He who began a good work in you will carry it on to completion until the day of Christ Jesus.*
>
> *Philippians 1:6*

Notes

[1]Major W. Ian Thomas, *The Indwelling Life of Christ: All of Him in All of Me* (Colorado Springs: Multnomah Books, 2006), 103.

[2]Ibid., 7.

[3]Ibid., 7.